Who's in the Mirror?

Other books in the Boys Town Teens and Relationships Series:

A Good Friend:
How to Find One,
How to Be One

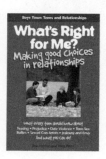

What's Right for Me:
Making Good Choices in
Relationships

For a Boys Town Press catalog, call
1-800-282-6657

Teens who are having problems with relationships, drugs or alcohol use, depression, parental conflict, or any other kind of trouble, can call the Boys Town National Hotline, 1-800-448-3000, for help at any time.

Boys Town Teens and Relationships

Who's in the Mirror?

Finding the Real Me

Ron Herron
Val J. Peter

BOYS TOWN, NEBRASKA

Who's in the Mirror?

Published by The Boys Town Press
Father Flanagan's Boys' Home
Boys Town, Nebraska 68010

Publisher's Cataloging in Publication
(Prepared by Quality Books Inc.)

Herron, Ronald W.
　　Teens and relationships/by Ron Herron, Val J. Peter. – 1st ed.
　　p. cm.
　　LCCN:
　　ISBN: 1-889322-19-9 (v.1)
　　ISBN: 1-889322-20-2 (v.2)
　　ISBN: 1-889322-21-0 (v.3)
　　　CONTENTS: v. 1. A good friend: how to make one, how to be one – v. 2. Who's in the mirror?: finding the real me – v. 3. What's right for me?: making good choices in relationships.
　　　SUMMARY: Teaches teens skills to enable them to develop self-esteem and healthy relationships with adults and other young people.
　　1. Teenagers–Conduct of life. 2. Interpersonal relations in adolescence.　I. Peter, Val. J.　II. Father Flanagan's Boys' Home.　III. Title.　IV. Title: Good friend　V. Title: Who's in the mirror　VI. Title: What's right for me

BJ1661.H47 1998　　　　　　　　158.1'0835
　　　　　　　　　　　　　　　　　QBI98–117

10　9　8　7　6　5　4　3　2

▼

● Italicized quotes are excerpted from "Ginger Snaps," 1976, and "The Spice of Life," 1971, compiled by Dian Ritter, and published by C.R. Gibson, Norwalk, CT.

Book Credits

Editing: Terry Hyland
       Lynn Holm
       Lori Utecht
Production: Lisa Pelto
Cover Design: Brian Wilson
Page Layout: Michael Bourg

Table of Contents

Introduction   1

Liking Yourself   3

Dating   31

Surface Beauty   45

Anorexia and Bulimia   57

Problem-Solving   65

Dealing With Parents   79

The Media   101

Being in Love   121

Choice and Change   135

Introduction

Many young people are not satisfied with who or what they are. Perhaps they don't like aspects of their appearance or struggle with their status or income. Some kids are unhappy with how they respond to certain situations. They make spur-of-the-moment choices, rush to find that perfect someone to fall in love with, or hurry to become an adult. These kids would like to change but don't know how to go about accomplishing it.

Where do you fit in, and how do you feel about yourself? The information in this book focuses on ways you can improve your self-image. It encourages you to make good decisions, strengthen positive feelings about yourself, and make the most of your abilities. This involves taking risks along the way, and taking risks requires courage. There are times when you will fail; however, if you continue to try, you are likely to

1

accomplish your goals. Don't be afraid of making decisions and taking some chances. Use the skills you'll learn in this book and you will be on your way to making the most of your life. Let's get started!

Liking Yourself

Have you ever gone through a house of mirrors at an amusement park? Each mirror is different and reflects an exaggerated image of your body. You can appear to be scrunched into a dwarf-like body or stretched like an enormous rubber band. You can look tall or short, fat or thin, or anything in between.

Mental images can be just as distorted. Some people see an exaggerated picture of their appearance or behavior. Many spend a great deal of time judging themselves. Some people tear themselves down, and others think too much of themselves. These folks let a distorted self-image get in the way of showing their goodness to others.

If you can see an accurate picture of yourself and look at the "total you," you're more likely to be able to take charge of your life and do the things that will make you happy. But it takes courage to be honest with yourself. Many people can't or won't look at their own behavior.

3

Who's in the Mirror?

Being able to take an honest look at yourself is a big step toward boosting your confidence, being more successful, and making your life more enjoyable. Look at yourself through critical but compassionate eyes. If you don't like what you see, you have the ability to change. That's a powerful idea. But you have to be motivated. You can't sit back and wait for good things to happen to you. You have to behave in ways that will make good things happen.

Domino's Story

Domino has a wide circle of friends. She thinks she is pretty well liked; she enjoys the friends she hangs out with, and they all usually have a good time together. But Domino would like to be able to stand more on her own, to know that she doesn't always have to think and behave exactly like her friends. She always worries when she buys clothes that they're not going to be just right. She pays attention to what the other kids say about music, movies, and TV programs before she makes her own choices.

Domino is also frustrated by her responses when she is with her friends. She doesn't have enough confidence to tell others what she thinks or wants to do. She's afraid her friends will think she's stupid, so she keeps her mouth shut.

4

*Domino's fear of expressing her o
gotten her into a couple of uncomfortable si...
tions lately. Domino is a good student – the
acknowledged "brain" of the group. Lately, her
friends have been asking for answers to homework questions or for help writing papers. They
have even asked her to cheat during tests. Domino
is uncomfortable providing this kind of help, but
she is afraid of losing her friends, so, against her
better judgment, she gives them help. Domino
sometimes goes with her friends to parties where
she is uncomfortable, and she doesn't speak up
when her friends talk about getting someone to
buy alcohol for them, even though she doesn't
want to have anything to do with it.*

*Domino would like to learn how to say "no."
She'd like to feel comfortable expressing her feelings in front of others and taking a stand that is
against what her friends think, but she doesn't
know how to go about it. Domino could use some
help with her confidence, self-esteem, and
assertiveness.*

Assertiveness

Assertiveness is a big word. It means being
able to express yourself confidently and positively. It means you can clearly and directly tell
someone your needs, thoughts, and feelings
without putting the other person down.

Being assertive is not easy. It takes a lot of guts, courage…and heart. There are many people who "clutch" or "choke" when they know they should stand up for themselves. Later, they curse themselves for not doing what they should have done. There may even be times when someone directly asks them for their opinion, but they refuse to share their true feelings. Instead, they say, "Uh, I agree with the rest of the group," or, "I don't know."

People who lack assertiveness let others run all over them. Why? They may be shy, self-conscious, or afraid of failing. Even though non-assertive people may realize that all people have a right to feelings and opinions, too often they just clam up and let other people make decisions.

Here is an example of being non-assertive: A telemarketer phones you and begins some lengthy promotional spiel for a product "absolutely guaranteed to make you rich." You know you don't want the product, but you don't interrupt or say anything. Or you timidly say, "I don't think that I need your product." Then the telemarketer comes back with a pushy sales pitch and you sit and wonder how you're going to get rid of this person.

Of course, the assertive thing to do would be to interrupt him politely and firmly say, "I'm really not interested. Please don't call again," and then hang up. But why do you think telemarketing companies are so successful? It's because many people can't say no. They listen to the whole presentation and ultimately buy the product, get put on a mailing list, or test something else on a "trial basis." Isn't it interesting that people can so easily be convinced to do something? Maybe it's because of shyness or a fear of hurting someone's feelings, but the odds are that people just don't know how to say no. The result: They buy something they didn't want.

On the other hand, there are aggressive people who push their way through life. Basically, they're insensitive to the needs of others. They may threaten, cajole, blame, criticize, or use any other bullying tactics that can get them what they want. An aggressive person may succeed in satisfying his or her needs, but no one wants to be friends with this person. Aggressive people may be expressing themselves, but it's at the expense of others.

Please understand that assertiveness is a world apart from aggressiveness. Don't confuse the two. Assertive people not only communicate their needs, but they also care about and respect the needs of others. That's entirely different from using aggression.

How to Learn Assertiveness

The first ingredient in being assertive is action. You have to do something to get going in the right direction. You have to start believing in yourself and your abilities. If you don't, you'll take a back seat to everyone, and they'll have more control over your life than you do. Learn to speak up confidently. Neither shy away from giving your opinion, nor try to force your opinion on someone. You have worthwhile opinions; they only lose worth when they're not shared with others.

Here are a few tips to help you be more assertive:

1 Start being more assertive with the people you like. Tell your friends how much you appreciate them and their help. Tell your parents that you love them and are grateful for all they do. By expressing your positive feelings to the people closest to you, you can learn to be more assertive in other relationships.

Give compliments to friends. Tell someone you appreciate what he or she did for you. Don't let good deeds go unnoticed. In fact, play a little game with yourself and see how many nice things people do for you in a day. You might be pleasantly surprised. Then, when you notice these things, speak up. Say, "thanks," or "I like that," or "that was a nice thing to do."

Telling someone you care is a big step forward, a step towards being assertive.

All of us would be famous if it didn't take any time, work, or thought.

2 **Learn how to begin a conversation.** Gather enough courage to be the first one to speak when you enter a room. Say "hi" to your teacher as you walk into the classroom. Ask someone a question. Beginning a conversation is assertive and shows a lot of confidence. Even if you're nervous, you can still start a conversation. For example, let's say you're getting ready to take a killer math test. You can say to the person sitting next to you, "I'm really nervous about this. Are you?" or "Did you study a lot for this?" Chances are you'll break the ice, and that person will say something too.

3 **Make "I" statements.** Accept responsibility for your own feelings and behavior. When you have an opinion that you think is worthwhile, be assertive enough to say, "I think..." and then state your opinion. Of course, someone might not agree with you and tell you so, but that is their right. You should feel good about having the courage to state your views.

This doesn't mean you strut around saying "I think..." all day. That is egotistical. Choose when you're going to be assertive. Never force your opinions on someone else or monopolize a conversation with your ideas. Other people like to talk too; conversation is to be shared.

Also, make sure your timing is right. Choosing to say an "I think" statement to the school bully could be hazardous to your health. Don't blurt things out or interrupt others. Remember: You're learning to become assertive, not aggressive.

Just as with the other skills we talked about, start small. Begin with situations where you can open up a little bit at a time. There are all kinds of opportunities if you just look. Gradually, you will feel more comfortable sharing your opinions with others.

What to Do When You Fail

In whatever you do, there is always the possibility that you may fail. When you do, realize that although your attempts at doing something failed, that doesn't mean you are a failure. Maybe you didn't plan carefully enough and jumped in too soon. Maybe you didn't have the resources to reach your goal. Maybe you set the wrong goal. But never call yourself a failure when you try to do something. Your attempts failed, that's all. Learn to accept it and get on with your life.

Success is picking yourself up one more time than you fall down.

So many people miss out on the wonderful world before them because they are so afraid of failing. They will never live up to their God-given potential if they don't allow themselves to try something new.

It is healthy to take some chances, reasonable risks that will help you be a better person. Know the good things that can result if you're successful. They should outweigh the bad things that can happen if you fail.

Sure, you're going to make some mistakes. You may feel self-conscious or embarrassed. But don't worry about it. No one likes to be embarrassed, but it shouldn't be an overwhelming fear. No one has ever died from embarrassment. Try to do something that will help you avoid being embarrassed in the future, but don't dwell on it.

People who try to do something and fail are infinitely better off than those who try to do nothing and succeed.

Please remember that everyone fails. Every famous and successful person on the face of this earth has failed. So why is everyone so afraid of failure?

One reason could be that other people have expectations of us that we feel we can't live up to. Although their intentions are probably good, parents, teachers, friends, and relatives sometimes have expectations that put a tremendous amount of pressure on a teenager. Or it could be that we put unrealistic expectations on ourselves. We set our goals too high and then get down on ourselves when we don't accomplish them. Whatever the reason, you have to remember that failing is part of life. No one can win all the time.

One of the keys to overcoming the fear of failing is attitude. Failing is not particularly enjoyable, but it can be a valuable learning experience. If you never try something because you are afraid you'll fail, you never learn to grow. You're not a failure when you don't succeed, only when you quit trying.

Many people who fear failure feel inadequate. They feel they just aren't as good as other people. Sometimes in an attempt to measure up and feel better about themselves, they turn to alcohol or drugs. They want to "loosen up" and let go of their insecure feelings. They think they can be funnier, more outgoing, or smarter. They end up doing things that make them feel worse. They kid themselves into thinking alcohol has the power to help them succeed. Actually, it just helps them fail again. Never turn to alcohol or drugs for a cure. If you feel like everything is hopeless, turn to someone you can trust to help you out. Don't turn to chemicals. They have no feelings for you.

❗ *Your mind is like a parachute. If you expect it to work, it first must be opened.*

Today's the Day

Start being more assertive today. Don't hesitate. Gather up your courage and go to it. You can learn to be more assertive, and you'll be much happier in the long run. Start slowly, and gradually work up to more difficult situations.

Here are some everyday situations where you can begin your personal assertiveness training. Remember that in all of these situations you are to be confidently assertive, not aggressive, and state your opinion in a calm, reasonable manner:

✔ Tell Mom and Dad how you feel about something you've never shared with them before.

✔ Ask a friend to return an item that he borrowed from you and never returned.

✔ Return an item of clothing to a store because it was defective or didn't fit. Explain politely to the customer service clerk why you want to return it.

✔ Say, "I'm not interested," to a telemarketing operator early in the phone call instead of waiting for the operator to go through the whole sales pitch.

✔ Start and maintain a conversation with a classmate at lunchtime, while walking to class, or when leaving school.

✔ Walk into a room where people are already talking, and say, "hi."

✔ Be the first one to state your opinion when a teacher asks for input from the class.

✔ If your food isn't done the way you ordered it, politely tell the waiter to take it back.

✔ Don't let a sales clerk tell you what to buy. Make your own decision.

✔ Give compliments or praise to a family member, then work up to a friend, an acquaintance, and finally to someone you hardly know.

✔ Give your opinions on general things like the weather, sports, or movies. Work up to giving your opinions on more serious issues.

Self-Esteem

All the experiences you have had in your lifetime contribute to your self-esteem. It's the general feeling of satisfaction (or dissatisfaction) you have about yourself. Your self-esteem started developing when you were very young, and it continues to develop as you mature.

Self-esteem is like your personal built-in computer. It takes in all the data around you – what other people say about you, the way they act toward you, the good and bad thoughts you have about yourself – and then produces an image in your mind. This image determines how you feel about yourself, good or bad.

The ability of human beings to think and feel is fascinating. We can look at ourselves and decide if we like what we see. We also can attach labels to our behavior: good or bad, right or wrong, nice or mean, friendly or stuck-up, legal or illegal, moral or immoral, and so on. The labels we put on our behavior also affect our feelings of self-esteem. For example, you can say to yourself, "I was very outgoing today. I joined in and said some funny things. I like myself when I act that way." You also can say, "I felt so stupid today. I wish I hadn't tried to be the class clown."

The more good thoughts you have about yourself, the higher your self-esteem will be. The opposite also is true; the more negative thoughts you have about yourself, the lower your self-esteem will be. Of course, these feelings can flip-flop, depending on the situation.

Can Self-Esteem Be Too High?

High self-esteem can be a negative quality when a person has the wrong kind of self-esteem. Some people who have high self-esteem aren't liked by other people. Too much of the wrong kind of self-esteem leads to conceit and self-centeredness. You probably know people in your school who think the world revolves around them. They are snobs, and they look down on other people. They are prime examples of too much self-esteem and too little compassion for others.

Taken to extremes, high self-esteem can convince people that they're special even if they are engaged in some kind of immoral, illegal, or antisocial activities. A bully can have high self-esteem; so can a thief, a drug dealer, a pimp, or a murderer. They all can convince themselves that they're good at what they do and can feel good about themselves, even though they harm others.

! *Conceit is "I" strain.*

Self-Respect

Self-esteem is at its best when it is coupled with self-respect. There is a difference between the two, but when they work together, they are a powerful combination.

Self-respect is based on your behavior; self-esteem is based on your feelings. Basically, it can be boiled down to this: Self-esteem answers the questions "How do I feel about myself?" and "How do I see myself?" Self-respect answers the questions "Am I making a positive difference in the world?" and "Am I giving or only taking?"

So you see, it is possible to have too much self-esteem. But it would be difficult to have too much self-respect.

❗ *People cannot be happy unless they feel their lives are in some way important.*

When you have healthy self-respect, you can see the good things you've done for yourself and others. It means caring and sharing with others, taking care of your responsibilities, and taking care of yourself.

Friendships and good relationships with others are fundamental in forming your sense of self-esteem as a teenager. If you can meet and make friends, you feel worthwhile and appreciated. If you don't have friends, you feel isolated and alone, and your self-esteem is damaged.

Self-esteem and self-respect are closely connected to what you accomplish in life. The better you feel about yourself, the more you are able to achieve; the more you achieve, the better you feel about yourself.

Having high self-esteem doesn't mean that you're perfect or that you'll never make mistakes. It does mean that you feel good about yourself, regardless of your mistakes and shortcomings. It means you know when you've messed up and you have the courage to change what you've done. To have high self-esteem, you must learn to accept and forgive yourself.

The worst thing that happens to people may be the best thing that ever happened to them if they don't let it get the best of them.

Low Self-Esteem

People with low self-esteem are lonely. Many are depressed. Some may try to put up a smoke screen with aggressive words and behavior, or they may blame others for their own weaknesses and faults. But the truth is they aren't happy with themselves. People with low self-esteem are easily frustrated. They may be violent, or they may avoid people and social situations.

Some people have a serious problem with self-esteem. They feel powerless and worthless. Their behavior is self-destructive. Many people who drink or use drugs, or who engage in promiscuous sexual activity or dangerous thrill-seeking, have low self-esteem. Teenagers with low self-esteem may fail in school and frequently get into trouble.

The self-esteem of suicidal people has hit rock bottom. They feel that their lives aren't worth living and that killing themselves is the only way to escape. If there is such a thing as hell on earth, it comes from hating yourself and your life. This hate is one of the most tragic feelings that a human being can have.

How do these negative feelings begin? Parents, relatives, teachers, coaches, and other adults can harm a young person's self-esteem. If these people frequently tell a child that he or she is bad, the young person will probably believe them and actually start doing bad things to prove them right. It's hard to feel good about yourself when someone you look up to calls you stupid, ugly, or no-good.

Some young people have low self-esteem because of frequent failures or inability to live up to the expectations other people have set for them. Failing, in itself, is not bad; in fact, it should be an encouragement to do better. But once a young person feels like a complete failure, it's hard for him or her to regroup and get back on the right track.

Kids who aren't liked by their classmates usually have problems with low self-esteem, too. Rejection becomes a way of life. Being an outcast pulls them deeper inside themselves and further away from other kids. The same thing happens to kids who are bullied. They receive the message that they are weak and deserve to be pushed around. That has a negative effect on how these kids feel about themselves; you can't feel very worthwhile when you've been told time after time that you are worthless. Children who are physically, emotionally, or sexually abused have very low self-esteem because they've been used by the adults who should have cared for them.

If you have a serious problem with self-esteem, and it has gotten to the point that life seems to have no value, get some professional help. Get it quickly. Don't allow self-destructive thoughts to make you their prisoner. Your life can change for the better. There is help out there. You can feel good about yourself. But you may have to rely on other people until you're strong enough to help yourself. If you think there is no one you can ask for help, call the toll-free Boys Town National Hotline at 1-800-448-3000.

Raising Your Self-Esteem

If you want to feel better about yourself, the first thing you must do is stop being your own worst enemy. Stop blaming yourself when you fail. Stop getting down on yourself when things don't go the way you would like. Raising your self-esteem will take some work, but you can do it if you're serious about improving.

▼ *People are generally about as happy as they*
● *make up their minds to be.*

Here are some strategies to help you feel better about yourself:

1 **Do a personal inventory.** Take a good look at yourself; don't pull any punches. Imagine that you are being analyzed by an outside observer. Be impartial and accurate.

Get a piece of paper, and draw a line down the middle from top to bottom. On the left side, make a heading entitled, "What I Like About Myself." On the right side, write, "What I Don't Like About Myself." Fill in each side.

Think about things such as ability to get along with others, confidence, academic strengths, athletic talent, musical ability, sense of humor, personality, hygiene, or appearance. For example, on the side where you list the things you like about yourself, you might write, "I'm a good friend," or "I help my parents around the house." On the side where you list the things you don't like, you might write, "I lose my temper too quickly," or "I don't try hard enough in school."

If you think you will have trouble coming up with examples, ask a friend, your parents, or another trusted adult to help you. Make sure you don't list more negative items than positive.

You can add new items anytime. For the next week, on the left side of the paper, write down a plus sign each time you do something you feel good about. Also, each time you improve in an area that is listed on the right side of the paper, make a plus sign.

See how many pluses you can accumulate in a week. This is a good way to see how many good things you actually do. Have a little competition with yourself. Try to beat your "plus" record each week. You can have fun with this as you raise your self-esteem.

This is your personal rating form. No one else has to see it or even know it exists. Each night, look at what you did that day; compliment yourself for what you did well, and vow to improve the other things.

❗ *Improvement begins with "I."*

2 **Learn to be assertive.** There are three basic ways to interact with others: aggressively, passively, or assertively.

Aggressive interactions involve attacking others. For example, someone gives you a little criticism, and you respond by arguing or losing your temper. Aggressive actions usually cause negative responses or retaliation from the other person.

Passive responses are just the opposite: You don't do much of anything. Other people are in charge, not you. Passive people just let things go. They don't make decisions or stand up for themselves. Avoiding others or not responding at all is a passive response. Being passive rarely benefits you because you don't let others know how you feel or what you want.

Assertive actions, on the other hand, can help you get what you want and let you express yourself in a direct and honest way. Being assertive can help you get what you want without hurting others or making a scene. Assertiveness is wonderful for your self-esteem. You actually stand up for yourself in a positive way.

Here are some tips on being assertive:

✔ Look at the other person. Eye contact shows confidence. Staring, however, can make the other person uncomfortable. Be sure to look at the other person in a way that shows you are interested and paying attention.

✔ Use your conversation skills. Know exactly what you're going to say and how you're going to say it. Know how loudly or softly you're going to speak, and what tone you will use to express your feelings. This will help you get your point across without being nervous or angry. Practice conversation skills in order to raise your confidence.

✔ Use appropriate body language. Have you ever had someone stand over you and talk while you were sitting down? It can be intimidating; it seems that the person who is standing has the upper hand. Try to be on the same level as the person you are talking with. Don't slouch or move from side to side or fidget; these behaviors may give someone the impression that you are not confident. Stand or sit up straight (but not rigidly) when you're speaking to someone else. Stand close enough to be comfortable, but don't invade someone's "space."

✔ Use appropriate facial expressions. A wrinkled brow indicates seriousness; a smile shows friendliness or sincerity. If you're giving someone a compliment but have a frown on your face, that person probably won't believe what you're saying. Practice: Look in the mirror and watch your facial expressions as you talk. Make sure your expressions match the message you want to get across.

3 **Learn to say positive things to yourself!** This is a big step toward developing a healthy self-esteem. Instead of cutting yourself down, build yourself up. Don't let that little voice inside your head say, "I can't do it" or "I'm so stupid. I'm going to mess up." If you let that voice continue, you'll eventually believe what it says.

You must learn how to encourage yourself. You need to make that negative voice shut up. Recognize when you're beginning to think negative thoughts, and stop yourself right away. You can do it; you can quiet that voice so that it doesn't make you think negative thoughts.

Tell yourself positive things. Tell yourself that you are a good person, that you will keep trying, or that you are going to remain calm.

Only when you begin building yourself up will you become self-confident. You may have had the habit of putting yourself down for a long time, so it might not be easy to change. But it will feel great when you finally do learn how to be your own best friend.

Practice right now. Say something positive about yourself. Say it over and over. When faced with a challenge or problem, say, "I can do this." When you have doubts or when you feel down, encourage yourself. Stress the positives. Don't say, "I can't." Say, "I can, and I will!"

 It is one of the most beautiful compensations of this life that we cannot sincerely help others without helping ourselves.

4 **Set yourself up for success.** Set some small realistic goals that you can accomplish. For example, maybe you have avoided someone because you were afraid of saying something dumb. Your first goal might be just to smile and say, "hi." Then do it. Afterwards, pat yourself on the back; it's a step in the right direction.

Start small, and keep moving ahead. You didn't just hop out of the crib and start walking. You had to learn by taking little steps and having little successes. And when you fell, you got back up and tried again. The same type of effort is needed in reaching any goals you set for yourself today.

Many people who fail to reach their goals soon quit setting any. But it's possible that they just set the wrong goals. They made them so hard or so complex that it was nearly impossible to succeed. Maybe they underestimated how much time and effort it would take to accomplish them. Or maybe someone else interfered with their plans. Whenever you don't reach the goals you have set, take some time to evaluate why. Don't just give up. Ask yourself what went wrong and what you could have done differently. Then start again.

Whatever goals you choose, set yourself up for success. Little by little, these small victories will boost your confidence. After you accomplish one goal, add another step to it. Make it just a little harder. You will be pleasantly surprised at the many things you can accomplish.

5 **Take responsibility for your behavior.** Don't blame other people. You are responsible for whatever you do, both good and bad. When things don't go as you would like, it's easy to say it was someone else's fault. Blaming others makes you look irresponsible.

If you make a mistake, correct it. Apologize, if necessary. Ask yourself why you did what you did, and then make sure you don't fall into the same trap in the future.

❗ *If you are willing to admit when you are wrong, you are right.*

For example, if you get a bad grade on a test, it isn't the teacher's fault. You could have studied more or asked for tutoring. If you oversleep, don't blame your parents for not waking you on time. Buy an alarm clock. If you get in trouble for being disrespectful to the school principal, don't blame someone else. Apologize, and accept the consequence without complaining.

Taking responsibility for your behavior is a big step in taking charge of your life. You will feel good about yourself when you realize that you are strong enough to handle problems on your own. What a wonderful gift to your self-esteem!

6 **Respect yourself. Stick with what you know is right.** Don't let others sway you with peer pressure and talk you into doing something for the sake of popularity or status. Doing something wrong hangs on your self-esteem like a lead weight; you have to live with the consequences, and you have to live with yourself. The decisions you make must agree with your values and your sense of what is right and important in life.

Let your behavior show others how good you are. Be friendly, helpful, and cooperative; that's what really counts. The way you treat others will influence the way others treat you in return.

7 **Help others.** Whenever you help someone else, you also help yourself. Nothing feels as good as being a good friend or neighbor. Help your friends. Do something nice for your mom or dad. Offer to help a classmate who is down or struggling with a problem.

Help people who are less fortunate. Visit a nursing home, work as a volunteer at the Special Olympics, or offer to help at a homeless shelter.

▼ *The glory in life is to love, not to be loved; to give, not to get; to serve, not to be served.*

Helping others will make you feel good inside. Helping others leads to a greater sense of self-esteem and self-respect because people like and appreciate what you're doing. You'll like it, too.

8 **Learn to solve your own problems.** Use the POP method described in the chapter on problem-solving to help you think of logical solutions to problems. Realize that you can make good decisions and gain more control over what happens to you. Decide how you can handle an ongoing problem, or make a plan for the future.

If you are unsure of yourself at times, ask a close friend or trusted adult for some advice. Listen carefully, and then make your own decision. Asking for help is not a sign of weakness; it's one of the best ways to learn. After you attempt to solve the problem, think about what you did right and what could be improved.

If you are given a task to do, make sure you understand exactly what needs to be done. People frequently make mistakes because they weren't assertive enough to ask questions that would have helped them complete the task correctly.

Show others by your behavior how special you are. Feeling good about yourself doesn't require some kind of physical self-indulgence such as taking drugs or having sex. You might feel happy for a little while, but it's a false happiness, and it doesn't last. Feeling good about yourself means feeling good about carrying out your responsibilities, living up to your moral standards, and helping others. It means doing what's right and being proud of what you've done. Show yourself how good you are, and others will see it, too.

▼ *Behavior is a mirror in which we all show our*
● *images.*

Dating

Dating can be a wonderful part of growing up. It allows you to develop new, special relationships. You learn more about other people, and yourself, in the process. You learn how to share your feelings and experiences with others. And you have fun.

Dating also can be a disaster. You're pressured to fit in, to be popular, to date someone who will treat you right. There are questions from Mom and Dad. You might worry that no one will want to go out with you. Someone you like might not pay attention to you. At the same time, there is an overwhelming need to talk, dress, and act like a "normal" teenager.

Many people have these concerns when they begin dating. Even though dating is an essential part of learning how to relate to the opposite sex, it doesn't have to be a cause for alarm. Let's look more closely at dating.

▐ Rick's Story

Rick has wanted to go out with Michaela for several months. He recently got up the nerve to invite her to meet him for a movie at the mall. He steeled himself, waiting for her to turn him down, but she said yes. He was excited – and nervous.

The big day came. Rick was wearing a new sweater he'd purchased just for the occasion. He and Michaela were going to meet at the food court and have a hamburger before going to the movie. He saw her sitting at a table with a couple of her friends, and as he was walking toward her, he tripped. He could see that the girls were trying not to giggle.

Michaela was already eating, so Rick went to the counter to order something for himself. He discovered he didn't have as much cash as he had thought, and he knew he wouldn't have enough for both a meal and two movie tickets, so he just bought a soda. He carried it back to the table and joined the girls.

Michaela's friends left to go shopping, and Rick got even more nervous. In fact, he was so nervous he spilled his drink all over the table. Fortunately, none of it landed on Michaela. He tried to start a conversation, but he felt like he was stuttering and saying stupid things. Sweat was dripping down his neck. Finally, Michaela *leaned over and said, "Why don't you just take a deep breath and relax. I'm nervous, too, but I really like you, and I'm having a good time." Then she smiled. The smile saved him – and it saved the evening, too.*

Not every kid is lucky to have such a nice person to date. In fact, some teens have a different picture of dating. The information in this chapter can help you choose a date who would be good for you.

What's It All About?

Dating should center around two basic goals: making friends and having fun. This may sound simple, but it can be extremely complex. Creating relationships is sometimes difficult.

Many dating problems are caused by inaccurate perceptions. For example, some people treat dating as a game, where winning means getting a date to have sex. When that happens, the original goals of making friends and having fun are forgotten, and selfish intentions take their place. The positive aspects of dating are lost. In the dating game, "players" can become manipulative and will do or say anything to win. That may be why the term "scoring" is used to describe sexual conquests. "Winners" become somewhat famous among their friends and get a reputation.

"Losers" are used, hurt, and rejected, and they may decide they don't want to take the chance of being hurt again.

In high school, dating sometimes becomes a popularity contest. For some kids, it's important to date someone who can raise their status. Other kids try to establish some form of identity by dating a lot of people. Some guys see dating only as an opportunity to score because they believe that having sex is the sign of a "real man." It can become so important that they'll even lie about having sex so their friends won't think they're "losers."

Like anything else in life, dating is what you make it. Treat it as a game and you'll find that people play by different, often unfair, rules; eventually someone ends up feeling bad when he or she loses. Treat it as an opportunity to make friends and have a good time – its real purpose – and you will find its true value and goodness.

As you grow and get to know more people your age, you'll realize that the best way to make a friend is to be one. And one of the primary ingredients of friendship is respect. If you and your dates treat each other with respect, dating will be the fun time it is meant to be. Without mutual respect, dating will be a failure.

Beginning to Date

Some teenagers seem to fit comfortably in relationships, while others struggle. Some teens date a lot, and others seldom date. That's okay. Some teens date at an early age, and others wait until later. That's okay, too. There are no age limits or numbers you should worry about. Your individual needs and interests – what's healthy and good for you – should be your guide. If you're a "later dater," don't worry about it. There's no rush. Dating should be a gradual process, just like when you meet anyone new and begin a friendly relationship. You shouldn't hurry the process along; let it develop naturally.

Many of your early "dates" won't be dates at all; you'll probably be with a bunch of boys and girls, just out having fun. "Group dating" is a good alternative to pairing off. Being with a group of companions or friends allows you to be more relaxed. You're not under as much pressure to impress one person. Group dating allows you to meet a variety of people in a variety of situations. Your social circle expands. You learn new ways of interacting with others and get glimpses of thoughts and opinions that may be different from yours. Get a group of kids together, and go to the mall or out for pizza, or over to someone's house, and you'll have a chance to see what others are like in social situations.

After getting to know someone better during group outings, the next logical step is to double date with a close friend. You can have fun and get to know your date a little better, but you still aren't alone with him or her.

Dating can have some awkward, nerve-wracking moments. That's common. When you begin dating, you risk getting your feelings hurt. It probably doesn't do much good to tell you that everyone goes through this, but it is the truth. You're going to make mistakes at times; that's part of the learning process of building relationships with other people. When you make a mistake, it's easy to feel stupid or embarrassed, especially when you wanted to make a good impression. But your dates will make mistakes, too. Learn to "shake it off." It's not a life-or-death situation. One of the best qualities you can possess is a sense of humor. Learn to laugh at yourself when you goof.

It also helps to know how to let your date off the hook when he or she does something embarrassing. If you're at a restaurant and your date spills water all over the table, say, "Hey, that's okay; let's clean it up." If you're at a dance and he or she stumbles, say, "It's all right," and keep on dancing. Don't draw attention to what the other person did. Put yourself in the other person's place. Other people will appreciate your ability to accept them without criticizing. That's part of the respect you should have for other people. You will find that they will respect and like you more because of it.

Usually, waiting until you're older improves the chances that your dates will go more smoothly. In fact, it may be a good idea to wait until you are a sophomore or a junior (or even later) to begin one-on-one dating. Some people even wait until after high school to begin regular dating. Dating and the complexities of relationships can cause a lot of pressure in your life, so it's wise to wait until you're emotionally mature enough to handle the stress that it can create.

Whom Should I Date?

Many tips for making friends will help you develop enjoyable dating relationships. Let's take a look at some of them:

1 **Find someone who is easy to talk with.** Few people are as dull as a date that has absolutely nothing to say or who talks about things that you have no interest in. Time crawls by. On the other hand, a date that is good at conversation is fun to be with, and time seems to fly.

One way to help insure that conversation flows easily is to date someone you already know and are comfortable with. Conversation with someone you don't know well can be stilted and uncomfortable. Even with someone you know, however, your first dates can be a little overwhelming. You may say something so dumb you can't believe it came out of your mouth. Even worse, you might "choke" and not have anything to say at all. That's normal. With every new experience, you're likely to make some mistakes. That's how you learn. That's why it's so important to start dating someone who makes it easy to carry on a conversation. You are less likely to feel self-conscious.

2 **Find someone who likes some of the same things you do.** This gives you something to talk about or an activity to do together. It's impossible to find someone who likes everything you like, but having some common interests can create a bond between you and your date.

3 **Find someone you're comfortable being around.** If you date someone who makes you feel inferior, your relationship isn't going to work. You will do things just to impress your date. That's phony. It's better to treat each other as equals, with respect and sensitivity. Remember: Dating is for friendship and fun, not game-playing.

4 **Find someone who is polite.** Good manners are always in style. While bad manners and disrespectful behavior might get a person's attention, they are lousy ways to get a date. Don't waste your time with someone who is known to make fun of others or who is sloppy and rude.

5 **Find someone who will respect your personal boundaries.** This goes for girls as well as boys. Don't allow someone to pressure you to do things you don't want to do. Force, whether physical or emotional, has no place in a healthy relationship.

There are hundreds of ways teenagers can get in trouble; you're well aware of that. Take the guesswork out of the relationship right away. Let people know there are some things you just won't do.

Dating Dos and Don'ts

Dating can be complicated. Here are some guidelines to help you establish your expectations – for yourself and for your date:

1 **Don't feel forced to date.** There may be some people who will try to rush you into the dating scene. Friends can pressure you to date someone in order to be part of the "crowd."

Some parents push their kids into dating by telling them it will raise their social status. These are poor reasons to begin dating. If you feel pressured to date, you're probably not going to have a good time. Sometimes a little nudge in the right direction is a good thing. But a shove into oncoming traffic is not helpful at all!

Some teenagers worry that if their friends are dating and they aren't, they'll be teased or abandoned. If these people are true friends, that won't happen. It's true that it can get lonely sitting at home when your friends are out on dates. Still, you should date because you feel ready.

2 **Don't look for a "perfect" date.** One of the values of dating is gaining knowledge and experience in making friends. As you learn more about dealing with other people (and more about yourself), you begin to form opinions of what qualities you will look for when you're older and want a more serious relationship. And those things will probably change as you grow up. Just think back to what you felt was important five years ago, and see how your ideals have changed. What seems important now will change as you get older. Don't search for perfection; you won't find it.

❗ *There can be no happiness if the things we believe in are different from the things we do.*

40

3 **Stick to the standards you have set for yourself.** Set limits on how often you will date. Set limits on showing affection so that you don't confuse your dates. If you do something that goes against your standards or beliefs just to get your date to accept and like you, you may not be acceptable to yourself. Stick with what you know is right. People who treat dating as a game might play by rules you don't agree with. At times, you may feel like a football referee, blowing the whistle to signal misconduct – "Offside!" "Interference!" "Out of bounds!"

For guys: When girls say "no," they mean it. Stop whatever you are doing that your date finds offensive. This isn't movie fantasy; this is dating reality. Your words and actions should convey respect, not manipulation or selfishness.

For girls: Guys may not understand the intent of your behavior. For example, you may think wearing flashy or sexy clothes makes you feel attractive or look nice. Your date may take this as a signal that it's okay for him to touch you or engage in sexual activity. Don't invite the kind of attention you don't want.

4 **Set some dating "guidelines."** These don't have to be strict rules, but it's a good idea to have certain details worked out in advance. For example, many dates are expensive.

Who is going to pay? In a traditional dating arrangement, the guy usually pays. (Some guys feel that a girl "owes" them something if they pay for the date. It's an obvious trap, and it's wrong, but it does happen.) Many people prefer to share the expenses; they decide to split the cost or simply pay their own way. Or maybe the girl pays one time, and the boy pays the next time. Whatever you decide, make sure that both of you agree with the arrangement.

Dates don't need to be so well planned that it seems as if you are following a script. But having a general idea of what you're going to do can relieve some of the nervousness. Answering the following questions may help you plan your dates so that you both have a good time:

✔ Are we going alone, or will we be with other people?

✔ Where are we going, and what are we going to do?

✔ What should we wear? Is the occasion casual, somewhat dressy, or formal?

✔ What time will we be home? Where can I be reached if someone needs me?

✔ Who is driving?

✔ What can we talk about? Do we have any common interests?

✔ How well do I know this person? Can I trust him or her?

✔ What do my friends think about this person?

✔ What can I do to stop being so nervous?

✔ What should I do if I'm not having fun?

✔ What am I going to do if I find out I don't like my date?

✔ What kind of reputation does my date have? Who are this person's friends?

✔ If we go out to eat, are my table manners good enough that I won't embarrass myself?

5 **Learn how to turn down a request for a date tactfully.** People risk being turned down whenever they ask someone out. That's hard to handle, especially if a person isn't over-flowing with confidence to begin with. If some-one asks you for a date, and you don't want to go, let that person down easily. He or she will undoubtedly feel rejected. Think of a kind way to say that you're not interested. Thank the person for asking, and gently refuse the offer.

If the person looks hurt, say something nice, but don't make excuses for your answer or change your mind out of pity. If the person per-sists or begins arguing with you, stick with your answer. In fact, feel good that you made the decision in the first place; this person can't accept "no" for an answer. On the other hand, someone may say "no" to you when you ask for a date. Accept the answer politely, and don't dwell on it.

Feeling comfortable on dates takes time. That's why these suggestions are important to think about. Even though there are no sure-fire answers to successful dating, there are some easy ways to avoid making a date a disaster. Be sure you don't play a "role," and act like someone you aren't. Don't come on too strong, and don't always expect things to go your way. And don't forget that dating is for friendship and fun.

All the social skills you learn from dating are valuable – cooperation, respect, patience, responsibility, honesty, and independence. Learning how to get along with others, including the opposite sex, will serve you well in your adult life.

Dating allows you to become much more aware of your values, morals, and personal identity. You learn how to protect them from being negatively influenced by others. All these experiences together will help form the adult "you." Absorb and filter the good things you learn from others, and add those qualities to your personality. You will find that there are no limits to how good a person you can be.

Surface Beauty

You are changing rapidly now – emotionally, intellectually, and, most obviously, physically. For some teenagers, physical changes become a major source of stress and worry. Although it's normal to be concerned about how you look and how you develop, your concern doesn't have to become fear or distress.

You are in an exciting time of transformation; you're leaving a child's body behind as you move on to adulthood. Just take a look at your school pictures or try on some clothes from two or three years ago to get an idea of how you've changed. It's amazing, isn't it?

The physical changes are obvious: You're probably getting taller and heavier, eating more, needing more sleep than you once did, and filling out. You're gradually growing into an adult. You're also changing emotionally. Some new emotions are connected to the physical changes that are occurring.

Who's in the Mirror?

This "growing up" time can make life seem much more complicated. Remember how simple life used to be? Now some things aren't so easy to understand. Besides feeling physically awkward, you might be feeling emotionally awkward, too.

All the changes you're going through can be tough to handle. This chapter will explore how best to cope with them.

▶ Jose's story

Jose is a kid whose growth has outpaced the rest of his classmates'. He has some acne, is kind of gangly, and the rest of his body hasn't yet caught up with his feet. The kids call him "Stork" and tease him a lot. But Jose hasn't let the teasing get to him. You see, Jose is a gifted young man, and he's confident enough to realize that his appearance is just a small part of who he is.

Jose is a good student, and he works hard to get good grades. He has set some goals for himself, including getting a scholarship to a university that he's had his sights on for some time. Jose doesn't wear designer clothes or dress to "in" standards. He has friends but doesn't really consider himself part of any particular group. He has lots of out-of-school interests, such as his job at a bookstore, his soccer team, and his family. Jose knows what's important in his life, and he's not going to let physical changes affect his feelings about himself.

46

No One Is Like You

All people mature at different rates. In general, girls start to mature earlier than boys. But each girl also matures at her own rate, just as each guy matures at his own rate. Some teens reach physical maturity early; for others, it takes longer. As a result, you may find yourself a year or two ahead of or behind your classmates and friends. This can cause some anxiety, so it's important to understand that everyone reaches physical maturity, but at different times.

The rate at which you mature is determined largely by the genes you have inherited from your family. If you are concerned with your rate of maturity, ask your parents about the physical make-up of both sides of your family. It is interesting to learn about your genetic inheritance. Treat it like the miracle it is. However, even within a family, brothers and sisters can look completely different; they can have a different body build, hair color, eye color, complexion, height, and weight.

Through all of these changes, there will be times when you don't feel good about yourself. You might feel gangly, clumsy, fat, skinny, or hairy. You may think that the whole world is aware of how you are changing. You may feel self-conscious, like a big glaring spotlight is shining on all of your imperfections. A pimple can seem as big as a football and bad hair days make you want to dig a hole and hide. You might feel embarrassed or shy, and it might be hard to be around other people.

Relationships

How you change physically can affect your relationships with others. Some teens want to avoid certain situations or people because they feel so self-conscious or embarrassed. They may feel angry that their bodies and looks aren't perfect; in fact, they might see more flaws than good qualities.

It's normal to think you aren't attractive to others because of all the changes you're going through. When you start thinking this way, it's easy to convince yourself that no one will ever want to date you. The truth is you can't continue to put yourself down and still expect others to be attracted to you. When you feel bad about yourself, it is reflected in what you do and say. People who are overly critical of themselves give off negative signals, making it easy for others to see what they are feeling.

> ❗ *A great deal of what we see depends on what we're looking for.*

Attitude!

So how can you feel good about yourself? The key to dealing with all these changes, and other people's impressions, is attitude. If you feel bad about the way you look, you'll probably feel bad about the total you. If you accept the way you look, you'll probably feel good about yourself in other areas as well.

While it's easy for someone to say "Think positively," it isn't always easy to do. You're going to get down on yourself at times or feel bad about the way your life is going. Your emotions may take a roller coaster ride of change – up one day, down the next – and you may feel them more intensely than ever before. Sometimes problems will seem overwhelming. They're not, of course, but if you haven't experienced them before, they can seem like a matter of life and death.

Teenagers, unfortunately, sometimes get teased about their bodies. If kids are teasing you, assure yourself that they're the ones with the problem. They lack sensitivity. Let their words bounce off you. People who tease you get satisfaction only if you react emotionally or feel bad.

Dealing with Changes

1 **The first thing to remember is that all teenagers go through times when they feel inadequate or unattractive.** It's normal to feel this way, but it can be unhealthy if you dwell on the negatives. These are perfect times to turn to your friends for some much-needed support. Get out and have fun with them, or do something worthwhile for others. It will make you feel better and get your mind off what's bothering you.

Be open enough to share your fears and worries with your friends. You may be surprised at how many times they have felt the same way. Support and encourage each other.

2 **Grow in all areas of your life.** Physical growth is just one part of becoming an adult. There are many other changes you will face. Your body may be growing by leaps and bounds, but to become a well-rounded adult, you must also develop morally, intellectually, emotionally, socially, and spiritually. Non-physical maturity often lags far behind physical maturity. For example, once teenagers reach puberty, they are physically capable of having children. That in no way means they are morally, emotionally, or socially ready to tackle the responsibilities that come with being a parent.

Concentrate on expanding the experiences in your life and doing positive things that can make you a complete person. You'll end up being a more responsible and happy person.

3 **Don't dwell on your physical imperfections.** If there are steps you can take to be more attractive, go ahead and take them. If there are things you can't change, learn to accept them, and make the most of what you have. Don't waste time wishing for better looks or trying to be someone you're not.

There's no one else exactly like you. Enjoy your uniqueness. It would be a pretty boring world if everyone looked the same.

4 **Take good care of your body.** Clothes, hairstyles, and makeup are ways to enhance your looks, but they don't have anything to do with being healthy. Your priority should be good hygiene and good grooming.

All those grooming habits you learned as a little kid are still very important: showering, brushing your teeth, wearing clean clothes, eating well-balanced meals, having good posture, and getting enough sleep. Respect yourself, and take good care of your body, and you'll not only look better; you'll feel better about yourself, too.

5 **Learn more about the changes your body is going through.** You're in a fascinating physical transition right now. Find out what's going on. Learn about puberty, reproduction, glands, hormones, and sexuality. Learn about proper nutrition and how it helps your body. Read about the harmful effects of alcohol and other drugs.

Find information in books, or ask an adult you trust. If you know what's happening in your body, you're less likely to be frightened or embarrassed. Think about the changes that are happening to you as miracles because they are.

❗ *That which is beautiful is not always good, but that which is good is always beautiful.*

Shopping for Identity

"Who am I?" "What am I good for?" Everyone wants to know the answer to these questions. Teenagers are especially curious. More and more they are told that the answers lie in a shopping mall, on TV, or in magazines. Most teenagers look to popular culture for clues about life.

What they hear shouts out the same message: Beauty can be bought! If you buy a certain product, your life will be wonderful. You're to wield your wallet or credit card like a gladiator's sword.

Shopping becomes more than a way to get the things you need; it becomes a quest for the meaning of life!

Teenagers are told that they have to look better than good; they have to look like the current media ideal. There can be no imperfections if you are to be truly beautiful. Unfortunately, teenagers have been overwhelmed by the "good looks" propaganda that appears in magazines, on TV, and in the movies. In advertisements, commercials, and celebrities, we see standards for popularity and attractiveness that few teens will ever achieve.

Not only teenagers are taken in; the same thing happens to adults. Thousands of them hope to buy a new and improved identity. They hop from one "miracle" to the next. Then they're disappointed when they don't look like the people in the ads. In the process, they worry and agonize over how they look and never really feel good about themselves. They are searching for something they will never find. In reality, no one can achieve physical perfection. What a blow to one's self-esteem!

There is nothing wrong with wanting to look good, and some products may help you achieve that goal. It's also perfectly all right to shop and buy nice things you enjoy. That's fun; it can lift your spirits and make you feel good. But don't expect a miracle. "Things" don't make you special in the eyes of others.

Some people resort to the latest fad without thinking of the long-term effects. Some teens go on harmful crash diets; some suffer from anorexia and bulimia – severe eating disorders, which can be life threatening. Some teens use steroids to pump up their muscles, an immediate way to bulk up their bodies. Unfortunately, the long-term results can be devastating; steroids are dangerous and should only be used under a doctor's supervision.

Take care of your body. Improve your body in healthy ways – exercise, get plenty of sleep, eat good food – but don't try to bring about immediate artificial changes. It's not worth it.

Feeling good about yourself should not be based solely on what you look like on the outside, but on who you are on the inside as well. It should be based on what you do with your life. There's an old saying that tells us "beauty is only skin-deep." This means the real beauty of a person is inside – the core of goodness that makes that person tick. All people have goodness inside; some just have a difficult time showing it because they're too caught up in how they think they're supposed to look.

The kind of person you are can be shown in different ways, by reaching out to help others, planning for a career, and doing volunteer work that helps make the world a better place. Cultivate the wonderful qualities of discipline, generosity, and loyalty. They won't be on sale at the mall, and they can't be bought with money. Concentrating on improving yourself by what you do, rather than what you look like, shows your real beauty. Others will notice.

So don't look for the answers to the questions, "Who am I?" and "What am I good for?" in the mall or in magazines or on TV. What you see in those places are just images. Instead, look within yourself to find your identity. To be truly successful, develop your mind through study; enlarge your capacity for friendship; explore new worlds through sports and activities.

Do the things that are good for you and your friends, and your true beauty will shine through.

▼ *What really matters is what happens in us,*
● *not to us.*

Anorexia and Bulimia

▶ Felicia's Story

Felicia's parents described her as a "perfect child." She obeyed her parents, got good grades, was in the school and church choirs, wore nice clothes, and was always helpful to those around her. On her thirteenth birthday, one of the girls at her party asked Felicia if she was gaining weight. Felicia was mortified! She was very concerned about her appearance and immediately thought she was fat and ugly. During the next few weeks, the mirror became her worst enemy. She convinced herself to go on a diet to "slim down." She knew that no boy would want to date her unless she was slim and had a "model's figure."

That decision led to constant turmoil; she couldn't think about much else besides losing weight. There was a continual tug-of-war in her head, waged by one voice telling her she was hun-

gry and another telling her not to eat. She went on a strict diet and started a strenuous exercise program. Her parents praised her for exercising and said it would really "fine-tone" her body. Soon she was barely eating. When she did eat, she felt guilty and worthless, and then criticized and punished herself for being so weak. She frequently felt sick, and her menstrual periods stopped altogether. She began missing school. Her clothes looked enormous on her. She always felt tired but still pushed herself to exercise. She avoided her friends; she felt angry and on edge.

One day, while exercising, Felicia passed out. Her parents took her to the hospital. She was diagnosed as having anorexia nervosa. The doctor said that she could have died.

Felicia had developed a deadly disease. She was starving herself to death, pushing her body and mind beyond the limits they could endure. However, Felicia was lucky. The disease was discovered in time, and with medical and psychological treatment, Felicia is expected to get better.

Types of Eating Disorders

An eating disorder causes harm to a person's physical and emotional health. Eating disorders can affect anyone, but teenage girls are the most likely to develop them. There are many reasons why people suffer from eating disorders, but at some point in their lives they developed an obsession with their weight. They may have wanted to look "perfect." They may have decided that being thin is the only way to be happy. They could have felt pressure to be slim – either real or imagined – from their friends or from society in general. Or they may have had a psychological or physical problem that affected their eating. Regardless of the reasons, people who develop eating disorders are in a dangerous and possibly life-threatening situation.

The two most common eating disorders are anorexia nervosa and bulimia. Let's look at both of these disorders and their characteristics.

Anorexia Nervosa

People with anorexia will do almost anything to control their weight. A strict diet is a likely first step. They may feel that if they can control their urge to eat, they have some power over their life. They may feel pleased that they are good at controlling their weight and their appetite. Don't think that anorexic people don't get hungry; they do. In fact, they are constantly hungry. Even though their bodies may be crying out for food, the anorexic person resists the urge to eat. This is completely different from a person going on a healthy diet to lose extra pounds. An anorexic person feels fat even though he or she may be very skinny. An anorexic's "diet" consists of very little or nothing at all. If they do eat, many anorexics will take large quantities of laxatives to rid their bodies of the food. Just as in Felicia's case, anorexic people are starving themselves.

Psychological characteristics of someone suffering from anorexia nervosa:

✔ compulsive and perfectionist behavior
✔ irritability
✔ inability to make decisions
✔ stubbornness, refusal to listen to others
✔ feelings of helpless and lack of control
✔ avoidance of others
✔ depression

Physical complications of anorexia nervosa:

✔ excessive weight loss
✔ cessation of menstruation
✔ constipation
✔ bloating
✔ yellowish skin
✔ hair loss
✔ muscle cramps
✔ lowered body temperature
✔ weakened heart muscle

It is possible to recover from anorexia nervosa, especially if the problem is discovered early. People who are in the later stages of anorexia face a more serious threat. They require hospitalization and intense counseling, and should participate in family therapy and a self-help group. Some anorexic people can benefit from using prescribed anti-depressant drugs. But the longer a person suffers from the disorder, the more serious and life-threatening it becomes. This can make total recovery very difficult.

Bulimia

Bulimia is characterized by what is called "binge eating." This means that a person goes through a period of uncontrolled eating – either eating all of the time or eating large amounts of food at one time. Usually, these out-of-control eating sprees are followed by forced vomiting. In other words, the bulimia victim tries to rid her body of the food she has eaten. Just like the anorexic, this person is preoccupied with weight, food, dieting, and body size. Many people who have bulimia feel bad about themselves, crave approval from others, and have difficulty handling stressful situations. Like anorexics, bulimics also may suffer from depression and want to avoid others.

The biggest difference between the two disorders is that anorexics constantly try to control the amount of food they eat, while bulimia sufferers feel that they have no control over their eating habits. The bulimic person usually goes through a destructive cycle: being hungry, feeling out of control, eating lots of food, throwing up or using a harmful amount of laxatives, and being hungry again. The result is malnutrition, hunger, and fatigue. A bulimic person may also suffer from heart irregularities, constipation, ulcers of the stomach and throat, dental decay, or a torn esophagus or ruptured stomach.

Although bulimia victims can recover completely, the physical complications are very serious. Bulimia victims need medical advice and psychological counseling in order to combat their disease.

The Effects on Family and Friends

Eating disorders are very difficult to overcome. Besides hurting the victim, they take an emotional toll on the victim's family and friends. When a victim's parents find out, they may be shocked or feel guilty, or feel they have failed their child because they should have recognized the warning signs of the disease. Brothers, sisters, and friends may feel some responsibility for what happened. They may feel they should have been more assertive and made the victim get help. The person with the eating disorder may strongly deny that there is a problem or go to great lengths to keep the disorder a secret. Whenever denial and secrecy are involved, it can cause a great strain on any relationship.

Family members and friends need to be patient and sensitive. Usually, the victim of an eating disorder will become angry that the "secret" is out and blame others for interfering. So the first step is to make sure that the victim feels the support and encouragement of family and friends. Victims also need to feel that they won't be looked down upon or criticized for having the disease. Friends and family members should talk openly with the victim and treat what that person says seriously. Of course, if the victim is at immediate risk because of malnutrition or begins making self-destructive or suicidal statements, it is important that he or she receives immediate professional help.

If you or someone you know is showing signs of any eating disorder and you don't know where to turn for help, call the toll-free Boys Town National Hotline (1-800-448-3000).

Problem-Solving

You make decisions every day. Some are simple, such as what to eat for lunch or what TV program to watch. Others are more important and harder to figure out, such as whom to date, whom to trust, or what you're going to do with your life.

As you grow and mature, you will face more decisions and problems. Some are sneaky; they appear harmless but then mushroom into major issues. How you handle them will make a big difference in your future happiness.

Unfortunately, some teens make the wrong choices. They often jump to conclusions, make the most obvious choice, or just wait for things to work out on their own. Look at your own life. Have you ever rushed into making a decision without thinking things through? Have you ever made a poor decision because you didn't have enough information? Most of us have. Not knowing how to solve problems effectively is a problem in itself.

Many people look at problems and solutions in a black-or-white fashion. Here are some examples of how this type of problem-solving works: A teacher criticizes your homework; you believe he hates you, so you drop the class. A girl you know messes with your locker at school, so you decide to trash hers, too. Someone invites you to a party. You don't have anything new to wear, so you decide not to go. With each of these situations, there are many options for solving the problem. Often, however, decisions are made in haste or frustration.

There is a simple method that can help you make better decisions. It doesn't take a great deal of time, and it works. This problem-solving method is called POP. The letters stand for Problem, Options, and Plan.

Let's look at each step.

Problem – Before you can solve anything, you have to know exactly what the problem is. This may sound elementary, but people often rush into making a decision before they've identified the whole scope of the problem. Sometimes they get caught up in their feelings rather than using logic. We all can make a "mountain out of a molehill" when we're upset or pressured.

The trick is being able to put your emotions on a shelf for awhile and look at a situation logically from many angles. That's tough to do, especially if you're really stressed when you're trying to make a decision. Anger and frustration can cloud your mind and make it difficult to see the problem clearly. If that is the case, you need to take a deep breath or find some other healthy way of calming down before you start looking for a solution.

Ask yourself questions that will help you piece together the whole problem, not just the obvious parts of it. Be like a newspaper reporter: Ask the "who," "what," "when," and "where" of a problem. Questions like these allow you to sort through your feelings and get a better picture of the whole situation.

Taking some time to think through a problem will keep you from acting impulsively. A decision made in haste often causes more problems, so before you do anything, know exactly what the problem is.

Options – Once you have identified the problem, think of different ways to solve it. Ask yourself, "What would happen if I did this? Or this?" Most options have advantages and disadvantages – positive outcomes and negative outcomes for each.

People may choose the first option that comes to mind or see only one solution and not explore other options that may work. They may think that the situation is hopeless, so they give up. Most of the time, you can come up with several ways to solve a problem if you take the time to think things through.

When you ask yourself what could happen, you are looking at all the possible consequences of each option. Why is it that sometimes an option works perfectly well and other times it totally bombs? It's because how well an option works depends upon the situation or the person you're dealing with and how well you carry out your plan. Although there is no way to know exactly what will happen, you can predict what will usually happen.

Think of all the things that could go wrong with an option, taking into account the situation or the person with whom you're dealing. Then think of what could go right. Do the positives outweigh the negatives? A solution is never perfect, but one option may have more advantages than disadvantages, so it's the one you choose.

Plan – After you choose the option that you think will work best, you need to decide exactly what you're going to do. This is your plan to solve the problem. The first two steps involve thinking; this step involves doing.

If the plan requires talking with someone, you may want to practice what you're going to say and how you're going to say it. If the plan involves completing a series of steps, figure out a workable method and time frame before you take action.

Let's look at an example of how the POP method can be used.

▶ Carmen's Story

Problem

Carmen has been invited to a party at a friend of a friend's house. Her friend, Renee, says the person who's having the party is a nice guy. Other people, though, have told Carmen that he's gotten in trouble for having loud parties where kids drink and get out of hand. Carmen also knows that a lot of kids she'd like to meet are invited.

What should Carmen do? Should she believe Renee and risk getting into trouble by going to a wild party?

Options

1 Say "no," and make an excuse. Carmen might tell Renee that she's tired or has other plans, or that she has to do something at home.

Possible positive outcomes? Carmen wouldn't have to go and run the risk of getting into trouble.

Possible negative outcomes? Excuses tend to lead to more excuses. Sooner or later, Carmen's friend will quit asking her to go to parties because she always has something else to do.

2 Carmen could go to the party and not tell her parents.

Possible positive outcomes? The party might be okay; no one would get in any trouble, and Carmen's parents wouldn't know.

Possible negative outcomes? The party might be terrible; someone might get into trouble; the police could be called, and Carmen's parents would find out and ground her.

3 Carmen could tell Renee she doesn't know the person well enough to go to a party at his house, and she doesn't want to take a chance of getting into trouble.

Possible positive outcomes? Renee might understand, and they both could decide to do something else.

Possible negative outcomes? Renee might not understand and might get mad at Carmen for not trusting her. Carmen might spend the night alone if Renee still wants to go.

4 Carmen could compromise with Renee. She tells Renee that she'll go, but that she's going to tell her parents about the party. Carmen will check to see if any adults are going to monitor the party. Carmen tells Renee that she'll go to the party for awhile, but if she feels uncomfortable, she will leave. If Renee doesn't want to leave, Carmen will call her parents to pick her up.

Possible positive outcomes? Carmen would still be able to go and meet other kids and still be able to leave whenever she wanted. Carmen would show Renee that she believed what Renee said about the friend giving the party, but she would have a "safety valve" in case the party isn't to her liking.

Possible negative outcomes? Renee might not want to compromise or want Carmen to tell her parents. Carmen's parents might not want her to go if no adults are going to be around.

Plan

Carmen chooses to compromise. She wants to go to the party to check it out. She feels she'll be able to tell if kids are drinking or if the party is getting out of hand. Carmen also decides to call her parents when she arrives and give them a phone number. She can make sure that adults are there, and she still has the option of leaving if she feels uncomfortable or if the party's no fun. The next time Carmen is invited to this person's house, she'll have a better idea of what to expect.

If you thought of other options, that's great. This example was used only to demonstrate how important it is to think things through before you make decisions. There usually are many ways to solve a problem.

Regardless of how old you are, POP provides a procedure for solving problems. It stops you from making hasty decisions and helps you arrive at a workable solution no matter the size.

POP also can be used for setting short- and long-term goals or making plans. Many small problems crop up every day, and POP is an excellent way to come up with solutions. Long-term goals could include deciding what college courses to take after graduation or beginning a savings account for a car or another large purchase.

Every choice you make affects your life in some way. It's logical that making good decisions will make your life smoother.

Exercise: Take some time to list several problems you're facing now. Use POP to come up with a solution. You will see how organized your thinking can be with this simple method of solving problems.

Problem:

Options:

Plan:

▼
● *The largest room in the world is the room for improvement.*

It's Not My Fault!

Any time you make a decision, you take a risk that something could go wrong. You can't be 100 percent positive that things will work out exactly as you planned them. An unexpected event or another person could throw everything off. Or another problem could come up that is more serious and needs immediate attention.

Sometimes you will fail. It happens to all of us. Don't let that stop you from attempting to solve problems in the future.

No one can be perfect. Most people realize this fact, but few want to admit it's their fault when they fail. Some want to push the blame onto others because many people think that failing is equal to being no good. That's not true. Every successful person on the face of this earth has failed. In fact, successful people fail many times. Babe Ruth was one of the greatest home run hitters who ever lived. He hit 714 homers. He also struck out 1,330 times, one of the highest strikeout totals in history. Was the Babe a failure? No way. He failed to get a hit many times, but he still was a great baseball player. In the same way, you can fail at some of the things you do and still be a successful person.

There's a big difference between failing and being a failure. Successful people succeed because they have confidence, set reachable goals, and have the courage to keep trying. Most important, they don't blame other people. Instead, they evaluate what went wrong and make changes as needed. Then they try, try again.

▼ *Failure is a temporary detour, not a dead-end*
● *street.*

Having the courage to make independent decisions is a sign of maturity. Achievement in anything – school, home, friendships, careers – is a result of a lot of hard work and learning from the mistakes you make. If you make a decision and things don't turn out the way you wanted, ask yourself two very important questions. The first is "Why didn't it work?" The second is "What could I have done differently?"

Look at your own behavior; don't point fingers and blame someone else for what happened. Maybe you didn't understand the problem well enough, or maybe it was more complex than you realized. Maybe you relied too much on how you thought someone else would act. Maybe you didn't look at enough options. Just remember: A failure gives you the chance to improve the next time. It doesn't make you a failure as a person.

▼
●
The problems of life are intended to make us better, not bitter.

When Not to Use POP

There are some decisions that should be automatic, some problems you will face that have only one healthy response, and that response is "no." If someone is trying to get you to hurt yourself or someone else, don't do it. Drugs, sex, alcohol, fighting, vandalizing – these are all harmful! The only wise choice is refusing to get involved with them.

Why is "no" the only answer you can give when these situations occur? Because they are wrong, and they can hurt you and others.

Perhaps the most important situation in which "no" can be the only answer is when a young person is thinking about suicide. Sometimes people get depressed and don't know how to handle tough problems. When they're really down, they don't think clearly. Sometimes they lose hope and think their problems can't be solved.

If you have ever thought about hurting yourself, please remember: There is hope, and there is help. Never let suicide be an option; it is a tragic, permanent solution to a temporary problem.

If you or someone you know is struggling with problems that seem too big to handle, get professional help immediately. Don't wait. If you don't know where to turn, call the toll-free Boys Town National Hotline at 1-800-448-3000, and counselors will find someone in your area to help you. They talk to kids all the time who need someone to help them when they're hurting. Counselors are on duty 24 hours a day, so don't hesitate to call the Hotline number if you or a friend needs help.

Whenever a situation is dangerous, illegal, or immoral, just don't do it. Decisions about whether to ride with a drunk driver or to take the pills another teen offers you or to beat up a kid from another school should be clear and automatic: Don't do it. The problems you will prevent far outweigh any criticism you might get from your friends for making your decision. There are some things that just aren't worth the risk.

If kids put you down for your decision, here's one way to handle it: Tell your friends that they made their own decisions and you made yours. Tell them they shouldn't condemn you for doing what you know is right. Be firm and consistent. Don't let them talk you out of your decision. Then tell yourself that you made the right choice and that you should feel good about it. It takes a tremendous amount of courage not to give in to the pressure others can put on you. Don't let other kids con you or flatter you or bribe you into doing something wrong. Stick by what you know is right and healthy and moral. It will make you a stronger and better person, and you'll be much happier with yourself.

You must face difficult problems head-on. Develop and use your problem-solving skills to make good decisions. Learning to think things through takes away some of the stress of solving problems. You won't have to "spin your wheels" worrying about what to do; you will have a plan of action.

 I am only one, but I am one. I cannot do everything, but I can do something. What I should do and can do, by the Grace of God, I will do.

Dealing with Parents

Has your relationship with your mom or dad deteriorated as you've gotten older? For many teens, getting along with their parents is a major problem. They say their parents nag all the time, don't understand them, and don't give them enough independence. Some even say that they can't wait to leave home because being away from their parents will solve all their problems.

If you ask some parents the same question about their kids, you're likely to hear complaints from them, also – their kids don't respect them, are irresponsible, or have a bad attitude.

It doesn't seem logical, does it? Shouldn't relationships get better as you grow up?

The answer to that question is "yes." But sometimes teens and their parents just don't see eye-to-eye. Later in this chapter, we'll look at several ways to improve your relationships with your parents. You may be living with one or both parents. Or you may be living with a stepparent or other relative, or another adult guardian. Every situation is different. But no matter what your situation, these tips can help you improve your relationship with the person or persons who are raising you. First, we'll look at what makes parents tick.

Parents spend the first 18 months of their children's lives teaching them to walk and talk, and the next 18 years telling them to sit down and shut up.

▐ Tysha's Story

Tysha is fifteen. Her dad has raised her alone since her mother left the family several years ago. Although her dad loves her very much, he is so protective of her that he questions every decision she makes. He has very strict curfews and lets her talk on the phone for just a few minutes at a time. He won't allow Tysha to date, even with another couple or group of friends.

Tysha and her dad have become very close over the years. They prepare the evening meal together and work together on the weekend cleaning the house and running errands. Tysha loves her dad very much, but she wishes she had a little more freedom, and she wishes he would trust her more. She's not sure how to go about talking to him about this problem; she and her dad could both use some help.

Understanding Your Parents

Like Tysha, things have probably really changed in your life in recent years. Not so very long ago, you looked to your parents to guide you and answer all your questions. You depended on them for just about everything – clothes, food, attention, love, discipline. Now, as you move toward adulthood, you don't rely on them in the same ways. You may question their decisions and disagree with their views. You may even rebel against their beliefs and ideas. You might think they're "out of it." When you were little, you probably loved it when your parents visited your classroom, ate lunch at school with you, or gave you a hug for encouragement. Now, you'd be humiliated if they did something like that in front of your friends!

❗ *Children are not things to be molded, but are people to be unfolded.*

First of all, let's cut your parents a little slack. They're not completely out of it. They are smarter than you in lots of ways. They may not be up on what's happening in music, movies, or fashion, or know what's hot and what's not, but that doesn't mean they aren't smart. They just aren't up-to-date on the same things as you. Just as you live in a teenage world, they live in an adult world. The two don't always exist in harmony.

Your parents have had more experiences to learn from, and not all of them were pleasant. When they remember the disappointments they faced and the mistakes they made when they were your age, they want you to do things better. They want you to be a better person. And even though you might not want to admit it now, you'll probably feel and act the same way when you have kids.

Parents worry. They know that there are a lot of dangers lurking in today's world. Look at what's happening out there – violence, gangs, drive-by shootings, drugs, alcohol, and abuse of all kinds. Parents wonder how you're going to cope with these things. They are concerned about your safety and pray that you'll make wise decisions.

They also worry about your future, your goals, what you're going to do with your life, and how you're going to pay your bills. More than likely, they struggled and are still struggling with the same things.

Let's face facts. Parents are people, too. That means they make mistakes. Most kids overlook that simple truth. But instead of forgiving them as they would a friend, some teens resent their parents' imperfections or throw their mistakes in their faces.

Why do negative feelings like this exist? On a very basic level, it's because teenagers see and understand more than they did when they were little kids. From the time a child is born, parents hold a position of dominance and authority. In a child's mind, parents do everything right. They have all the answers, and what they say is etched in stone. When a child becomes a teenager, it may be an unpleasant surprise to find that his or her parents are imperfect and weak sometimes.

Parents fail. They sometimes make bad decisions. They get depressed and angry and upset. And they have needs, just as teenagers do. They need to feel important, be true to their beliefs, have friends, and have fun. When these needs aren't met, they aren't happy, just like teenagers, just like all human beings.

 Adolescence is that period when children refuse to believe that some day they'll be as dumb as their parents.

As you grow up, your parents also struggle with your new position in their lives. It isn't so much that they struggle with your need for independence; they probably remember having the same need when they were teenagers. What might bother them is the way you show your need for independence. They might feel that you sometimes rush into things and fail to realize how vulnerable you are to society's dark side.

Take some time to think about the way you handle their criticism now. Do you keep your cool and respond maturely, or do you argue and yell like a little kid throwing a tantrum? Do you condemn their opinions or calmly disagree? This isn't pointing fingers at teens. Many parents haven't reached the stage where they can handle their emotions in a mature manner, either. But remember: This is about your behavior and how you can make your relationship with your parents better. The way you respond will determine whether you have a relationship that is compatible and happy or one that is full of hard feelings and conflict.

Teenagers have a tendency to believe they are invincible, that their youth and enthusiasm are enough to carry them through anything, and that bad things always happen to someone else. It's not true. That attitude is dangerous, and parents realize this. Teenagers are a high-risk group. That doesn't mean that teenagers are bad or irresponsible. It only means they are experiencing and learning things they've never experienced before, and whenever anyone is faced with something new, mistakes are likely to be made.

Let's look at several examples. A young boy wants to help his father with a cookout, so he asks if he can light the grill. The father really likes the fact that his son wants to help, but he says "no." The kid becomes very upset! He was just trying to please his dad, and now he feels reject-ed. But the dad did the right thing. A responsible father is not going to let his son try something he isn't ready for because the father doesn't want the boy to get hurt. What Dad should do is ask his son to help him in another way (cleaning the grill or pouring the charcoal), and then show him how to light it. That's teaching through model-ing. Dad monitors and teaches one step at a time until he thinks the child is ready to try it on his own.

Another example involves a skill teenagers want to master. All teenagers want to drive, right? What a feeling of exhilaration, power, and freedom! But you can't just hop behind the wheel and begin driving. It's dangerous. There is too much to learn. No adult should ever allow you to drive a car without lots of practice. Driving is a complex skill. It requires repetition. You learn a little more each time you drive. Your parent or the driver's education instructor gives you tips as you drive, and you become slightly more com-fortable each time. As the experiences build, you become a better and more responsible driver.

Now, take these two examples and connect them to other aspects of your life – going to work or school, using machinery or appliances, going to parties, dating, going to new places on your own. Do you see why your parents are cautious about the new things you want to do? Some of the problems you face are as obvious as big chuckholes in a poorly maintained street. Others lurk beneath the surface like land mines. You don't know they are there, but your parents do because they've traveled that road before. Benefit from their experience. Ask them questions about the ways they would handle the problems you face. Open the door to your world, and let them walk in.

Let's look on the other side. You deserve some breaks, too. If you don't take some chances, you'll never learn. But the risks you take should be reasonable, and you should have your parents' support and guidance. The sad reality for some teens is that at a time when they should be able to rely on their parents, they are at odds with them. If this is what's happening in your family, there is hope. Things can change for the better, and the suggestions at the end of this chapter can help.

Problem Parents

Try as they may, parents are going to make mistakes. Some parents love their children so much that they don't allow them to grow up. They spoil and overprotect their kids. That can be very unhealthy.

On the other hand, some parents give their kids too much freedom. They allow them to stay out late, shirk responsibility, and get involved in activities that are not age-appropriate or safe. They are overly permissive and let their kids do too much of what they want. The teenagers may think this is wonderful for a while, but they eventually get into trouble because they have no direction or discipline.

Rules and discipline lead to security and self-confidence, and they should be close friends, not enemies, of growing up. Take them away, and you have confusion and chaos. The trick is learning how to grow up and gain independence within your parents' rules, not in spite of them.

There are other types of problem parents. They can be harsh and severe and forbid their teenagers to do normal teenage things. They can be inconsistent, allowing their teen to do something one time but not another. They can be prejudiced and closed-minded. They can be old-fashioned and set in their ways, often failing to see the good in their children's generation. They can make fun of their kids – their clothes, their hairstyles, and their attitudes. They can set unrealistic expectations that their kids can never fulfill, and then complain when their kids fail.

Unfortunately, there are some parents who just don't or won't live up to their duties. This is a terrible problem that will certainly lead to problems in other relationships. In these cases, professional help is needed. If you or a friend you know is in a situation like this, please don't hesitate to call the Boys Town National Hotline, 1-800-448-3000.

For the most part, however, the problems parents may have are not so severe that you can't do something to help them, and these are the situations we'll address in this chapter. Maybe you can't make everything perfect, but you can make some things better. You can help your parents be better parents. You can change them. That's right. It sounds kind of funny, but you actually can make them better parents through your behavior.

The skills in this book can help. Learn how to solve problems. Learn how to have a conversation with your parents that doesn't turn into a debate or a yelling match. Learn how to ask for help. Compliment your parents; thank them for the things they do for you, and tell them you love them. Demonstrate your positive feelings. Taking this kind of active approach to your family's situation will help your parents and make you feel better about yourself, too.

▼
● *We may give without loving, but we cannot love without giving.*

A Change for the Better

Teens and parents usually have the most problems when they don't share their feelings with each other and when they refuse to compromise. It doesn't matter who is at fault – both sides may be wrong to some extent – but it is important that parents and teens learn to communicate. It's not a simple task, but it can be done. If both sides aren't willing to talk, they harbor negative feelings or blame one another and nothing gets solved. That can get ugly. It can create a vicious cycle that never stops spinning out bad feelings.

Part of the problem stems from the fact that teens feel a need for independence. They want to do more things on their own than their parents think they can handle.

Please realize that you will never be totally independent from your parents. They will always be your parents, and they will always do "parent things." Your goal should be to become interdependent, relying on one another in a mature new way. You should strive to have a mutual respect for and dependence on one another. In the adult world, you will help them and they will help you. You will share thoughts, feelings, and attitudes more than ever before. Although right now you may feel that a relationship like that will never happen, it can. And when it does, it's a wonderful and rich experience.

There are some steps you can take right now to help your parents realize how responsible you are. They will help you begin to build a stronger, better, and more adult relationship.

1 **Set a time to be home, and stick to it.** This develops trust. Mom and Dad are more likely to be flexible if they can trust you to get home on time. When you're late, it irritates your parents and makes it appear that you don't care or are irresponsible. So, if you say you're going to be home at a certain time, make sure you are.

If you aren't home by the time you said you would be, your parents will probably react in one of two ways – worry or anger. You could be at the safest place in the world, but only you know that; your parents don't. They have no idea what's happening.

2 **Check in.** If for some reason you're going to be late, let your parents know. If your plans change, tell them. Use a pay phone, if necessary. It's a small price to pay. Not only will you ease your parent's worries, but you'll also save yourself a lot of hassles and explanations. If for some reason you can't phone them, let them know where you were as soon as you get home. Tell them where you went, what you did, and why you couldn't call; it could head off a lot of trouble.

When you get home, don't head straight for your room; talk to your parents. Avoiding them raises a red flag in their minds. Tell them what you did. Not only does this help alleviate some of their curiosity and suspicions, but it also helps you avoid being questioned. Teenagers sometimes feel like they are being grilled by the FBI when their parents ask them what they were doing. Take the initiative by starting the conversation, and you'll find that they'll ask fewer questions. In addition, parents get annoyed when they ask their teen what he or she did and they hear, "Nothing," or "We were just hanging out." You don't have to give them a detailed description, but take the first step: Tell them what you did, and the confrontations that lead to bad feelings can be avoided.

3 **Keep your promises.** If you said you would clean your room before you leave, do it. If you promised to fill the car with gas before you get home, make sure you fill it. If you're asked to do something for Mom or Dad before you leave, do it right away. You never know when you'll get a call, when someone will drop by, or when something else will happen that keeps you from doing what you said you would do. One of the most frequent complaints parents have about their kids is their lack of responsibility. Keeping promises not only shows a great deal of maturity and develops trust; it also shows how responsible you can be.

4 **Put aside some time for Mom and Dad.** Your friends are important, but so are your parents. They also can be great friends if you give them a chance. You don't have to spend huge amounts of time with them, but at least let them know what's going on. You can say a lot in a few minutes. Don't leave them guessing about what's happening in your life. They may jump to the wrong conclusions; parents are just like that.

When was the last time you had fun with your mom or dad? Do some of the things you used to do as a kid – play a game with them, reminisce about good times, or watch a TV show or movie together. Having fun together is a bond that carries over into other areas of your life.

Give your parents a glimpse into your world. Tell them about things that happen in school and with your friends. Introduce your parents to your dates and tell them something about the people you're dating – what their interests are, where they live, what their parents do, and so on. Parents feel uncomfortable when they never see the people you're going out with. One other thing: Once in a while, tell your mom and dad that you love them.

5 Share your feelings. Sometimes, parents simplify your mood; they boil it down to being mad or depressed. But you have a wide variety of feelings and emotions. It will help them understand you if you can describe them clearly. This will help you avoid questions like, "What's wrong with you?" and "Well, why didn't you tell me what you were feeling? I'm not a mind reader." If they have to guess how you are feeling, it's likely that they will guess wrong. That can lead to more questions or negative statements or consequences. Then you or they feel irritated or upset. It's simpler to tell them what's going on.

Tell them how you are going to handle a problem at school, on the job, or with a friend. Even if you think that their reaction will be negative, have the courage to speak up. This shows them that you want to be more in control of your life – that you are actively doing something to be more responsible. But make sure you bring up topics in a calm manner. That's a key to having them listen to you. Many times, parents react to the way you say something rather than to what you say.

There's nothing wrong with telling your parents when you're depressed, anxious, or frightened. Guys, in particular, often hesitate to describe what they are feeling because they think it takes away from their masculinity. That's not true. You can be a man by talking about what you feel. It is a mature and healthy thing to do.

If at first you meet with a little rejection, or if your parents downplay your feelings, don't give up. If they say, "Oh, that's nothing to worry about. Wait until you grow up. Then you'll know what problems are," don't overreact, say something sarcastic, or get mad. Remember: You're trying to change their behavior and their image of you. You can teach an old dog new tricks; it just takes some time. Keep trying.

Be sure to recognize and thank your parents for the times when they do listen or when you feel that they accept what you're saying. Recognize even the smallest improvements that they make. You may be surprised at what happens. They may listen to you more and may be more accepting of your feelings. They even may share some of their feelings. These can be great rewards. Even if everything doesn't turn out exactly the way you want, it's going to be better than it was before. It's certainly worth trying.

These are opportunities to let your parents know what life is like for a teenager today. Show them how mature you can be.

6 **Admit your mistakes.** This scores huge points with parents. Instead of making excuses when you mess up, calmly say that you made a mistake. Face the music. It's as simple as that. If your dad or mom criticizes or scolds you for what you did, don't respond angrily.

If you break or ruin something, offer to pay for it. If you don't have the money to buy whatever it is you damaged, offer to do jobs around the house as payment. If you get in trouble at school or get a low grade in a class, be honest. Don't say that the teacher hates you or that you never get any breaks. Even if it's true, parents will usually look at it as an excuse. Why? Because you can always take steps to improve the situation: You could have studied more or gone to someone for help. Take responsibility for your own behavior. Say you messed up, and tell them what you're going to do to improve.

Admitting your mistakes doesn't mean you meekly say you're wrong every time a problem occurs in your life. Sometimes there are legitimate reasons for a bad result. If you're blamed for something you didn't do, be assertive and calmly ask what happened. Don't be a scapegoat. Regardless of the situation, if you take responsibility for your own behavior and tell the truth, you'll be light years ahead of most people.

Even if your parents don't accept your explanation, you must stay calm; this will allow them to see you in a different light. Don't argue or make negative statements. They will realize that you can stay calm and won't blow up every time something doesn't go your way. They will see you as mature and able to take responsibility for your behavior. You may have to be more mature at times then they are. If they are yelling, keep your cool. Don't get into a shouting match with them. Talk about impressive! Most parents would do cartwheels if their teenagers acted like this!

7 Accept consequences. Whenever most parents think their teenager has done something wrong, they respond with a consequence of some kind. Few ignore the opportunity to teach their son or daughter "a lesson." Accepting a consequence is one of the toughest things for teenagers to do. And it's a major cause of arguments and turmoil in many families.

You must first avoid making matters worse by arguing or getting angry. You may feel upset, but for now, practice self-control. Striking back or refusing to accept what they say will not take the consequence away; it is likely to increase it.

Once parents are upset, they rarely stick with the original consequence; usually they keep adding to it. For example, let's say your parents grounded you for a weekend. You argue with them. They respond with, "Okay, make it a week." You tell them how unfair they are. They call you disrespectful and ground you for a month. And so on. See what happens? Remember: Don't make the situation worse by arguing or being as upset as they are.

You have to adopt the attitude that this isn't the clash of the Titans, where you will fight each other until one gives in. Instead, you have to learn to get what you want in acceptable ways – by staying calm, listening, and accepting what comes your way. That's tough to do, isn't it? You might resist this notion, but please give it a try. And remember that these behaviors also will help you in many future situations. Think of it this way: If you were on a job and argued with your boss every time he or she gave you criticism or extra work, you wouldn't keep your job very long. If you learn to accept consequences appro-priately, you'll have opportunities to explain yourself later. You can take some of the unfair-ness away by practicing self-control at the moment and working on fixing the problem later.

If you really feel the consequence was unfair, there are four things you might try:

✔ Come back later, and state your reasons. The reasons you offer when you first get the consequence may be treated as an excuse or arguing. Give your parents a chance to cool down. Then explain why you think the consequence was unfair or why they may have misunderstood the situation.

✔ Ask if you can compromise or negotiate. Possibly, you could have a different consequence, or you could reduce the one you received. For example, if you were supposed to be grounded on Tuesday, you could ask to be grounded on a different day or ask to have a friend over instead of staying home alone.

✔ Ask your parents what you should have done, or ask how they would have handled the situation. Find out what they want you to do so you can avoid a consequence like this in the future. This works well with parents who always want to feel they are in control. You are asking them for advice, and they appreciate that.

✔ If you feel there is no way that your parents will listen to your reasons or compromise, say, "I understand what my consequence is. I don't agree with it, but I understand why you think it's necessary." Then leave it at that. Again, staying calm is of the utmost importance. Even if you feel like you were stuck with an unfair consequence, staying calm increases the likelihood that your parents will view you as mature and responsible. It's hard to tell yourself that when you feel you've been treated unfairly, but it's true. You can turn these situations into ones that may benefit you in the long run.

8 Do good things. Take charge of your life so that you can make a difference. Do good things. When your life is finished, people should think that the world is a better place because you were around. Mark Twain once said, "Endeavor to live so that when you die even the undertaker will be sorry." In other words, we're all put on this earth to do good things. We're called on to join hands with our friends and family in what our nation's founders called "the pursuit of happiness." They didn't mean scouting for parties or indulging yourself. They meant making the world a better place through the way you live your life. It means helping others live better also.

What does all this have to do with parents? They see you as an extension of themselves. They want you to do good things and be a responsible citizen. What you do with your life is as important to them as what they do with theirs. Making a positive difference shows how much you value what they have taught you, and it's an excellent way to show how much you love them.

 Many parents are so anxious to give their children what they didn't have that they neglect to give them what they did have.

One thing is certain: However much or little your parents demonstrate their love for you, they do love you. Maybe they show it in ways you don't like or understand, but you will always be their child. The tips in this chapter might help you understand them a little better and might even make your family stronger. Maybe you will be successful in changing some of their behaviors toward you. But more than that, you can begin to build a new, adult relationship with your parents. They can become your lifelong friends. Listen to their advice. Develop their trust. And don't be afraid to comfort them when things aren't going well in their lives.

Making something of your life is a big part of your relationship with your parents when you are growing up. Show them that you can handle your responsibilities reliably and maturely. Show them that they can trust and depend on you, and that you can make good decisions.

Lofty goals. Corny? They shouldn't be. They should be the goals you live your life for.

The Media

We live in an information age. Every day we are drenched in a media downpour. Images, sounds, ideas, and sensations zap us at lightening speed. Sometimes it's difficult to take in all of the information before we're hit with another burst of new ideas.

Have you ever thought about the effect the media have on us? This is a controversial topic today. Parents and educators are especially concerned about how harmful media messages are to children.

It's safe to say that the media are neither all good nor all bad. On one hand, the media allow us to explore a wonderful world full of excitement and discovery. We can learn and experience fascinating new things. On the other hand, there's a media world that is negative and twisted, full of harmful messages that some people believe.

The bombardment of messages starts when we're very young. Look at the number of television commercials that hawk toys, breakfast cereals, and candy. How do these ads affect kids? They make products attractive to the point where small kids whine and throw temper tantrums in stores because they want what those cute kids in the commercials have. At a very early age, children's attitudes are influenced by the media; they're being told what they should play with, eat, and wear. Even more disturbing is the idea that they're being told how to think. The media have a powerful impact on young children.

Teenagers also are a major target group for the media because they are such a big buying group. Business people greedily anticipate how much money they can make from a product that is a hit with teenagers. Teenagers spend millions of dollars every year on tapes and CDs. They go to movies, rent videotapes, attend concerts, and spend millions more on clothes. They watch TV and listen to the radio by the hour, which is why the majority of youth-oriented advertising is found in those media outlets.

▐ Shanda's Story

Shanda, like most kids, has done her share of watching television. Without giving it much thought, she's internalized the messages she's received from advertisers, music videos, and pro-grams. Unfortunately, the result of this internal-ization has been Shanda's dissatisfaction with herself. She decided at some point during the years of watching "perfect" bodies parade across the screen that she didn't quite measure up.

Shanda is 5 feet 7 inches tall and weighs about 125 pounds. Of course, Shanda would never admit that to anyone, because even though her weight is on the lower end of "normal" on her doctor's chart, Shanda is convinced she's fat. She also thinks that her hair is the wrong color, her nose is too big, and her jaw is too square. Shanda is on a perpetual diet and is convinced that with just a bit more exercise and dieting, her body will finally be the right size..

Shanda wouldn't think of buying clothes with the "wrong" label. She spends all of her allowance on clothes and products to make her look better, and she nags her mom for spending money as well. Shanda's mom doesn't have much money to spare, but she's bought Shanda's story that she won't fit in if she doesn't have just the right look. Shanda is obsessed with her appear-ance and spends hours looking at herself in mir-rors. She colors her hair, buys expensive jewelry, and wears heavy makeup and perfume. But she's still not satisfied, and lately she's begun begging her mom to let her have surgery to "fix" her nose.

Shanda's in trouble. She's bought the messages that the media have bombarded her with: What's important is not what's on the inside, but how you look on the outside. She's neglected to develop her inner beauty while chasing an ideal of physical beauty that she'll never achieve. What she doesn't realize is that unless she changes her focus, she'll never be happy with who she is.

Advertising

The goal of this chapter isn't to condemn the media, although we will discuss their obvious negative qualities. The goal is to make you aware of the methods the media use to get people to buy what they are selling. Once you are aware, you can make logical choices about what to buy and what not to buy, what to believe and what not to believe.

Basically, the media sell two things – products and messages. We are told to "buy" not only a product but also an idea or a lifestyle. Let's start with advertising. The whole trick in advertising is to get people (consumers) to believe that their lives will be better if they buy certain products. The media use peer pressure and a constant barrage of words and images that are focused on trying to get you to buy.

This isn't necessarily a case of false advertising; there are some very good products on the market. Many of them do improve our lives in some way. But many people, especially kids, start believing that they must have the product. They are gradually brainwashed into thinking that a product can bring about dramatic changes in their lives, and transform them into whatever they dream of being. When people are convinced that a product is a necessity, problems can follow.

Here are some claims, obvious and subtle, that some advertising makes:

✔ Use this product, and your life will be easier; hassles will vanish.

✔ If you don't use this product, you'll be left out or ridiculed.

✔ Use this product, and you'll be more handsome or beautiful, and all of your flaws will disappear. Use this product, and you'll be sexy and popular.

✔ Famous, successful people use this product, and it has made their lives wonderful. If you use the product, your life will be as wonderful as theirs. In other words, this product is one reason this person became, or stayed, famous and successful.

✔ Using this product will create excitement and exhilaration far beyond your experience.

✔ This product has been "proven" in scientific tests to bring about fantastic results.

In addition, electronic advertising uses high-tech computerization, visual images, or songs that stick in the consumers' minds and make them think of, and eventually buy, the product.

A Media Advertising Exercise

While watching TV or reading your favorite magazine, see if you can determine which of the advertising methods we just discussed is being used. Here are some products to think about:

✔ Clothes
✔ Food
✔ Drinks
✔ Colognes or perfumes
✔ Cosmetics
✔ Skin care products
✔ Hair care products
✔ Cars
✔ Movies, CDs
✔ Games

Ask yourself: Who is the audience? What is the message? Does this message make me want to buy this product? If not, who is the target audience?

Have some fun with this. It's all right to enjoy commercials and other advertising, but you should never let these ads convince you that a "miracle" is going to happen if you use a certain product. Too often, that's what advertisers want you to think.

Media Messages

Various forms of the media – books, magazine, movies, TV shows, music – also try to sell something called image. In subtle and not-so-subtle ways, they try to tell you what should be popular and what should be ignored.

The problem is some people believe the hype and let it influence their lives much more than it should. They become mesmerized by the images and begin to mimic what they see and hear. Kids in particular are information sponges. They soak up all of the messages and images that surround them, often without understanding what they mean. Kids and teenagers are great imitators; they pick up "the walk" and "the talk" from the people or things that present the images, both good and bad.

Another problem stems from images that are intended for adults but are unleashed without restriction, so that anyone can see or hear them. Adults may be able to see through the gimmicks and make good choices based on experience, but some young people may be easily influenced. Those adults decide to turn off the TV, forego buying the CD, walk out of the movie, or decline to subscribe to the magazine.

Even worse are the sexual or violent messages or images that can negatively affect children and adults. We'll discuss those in the next section.

How Far Can It Go?

Of all the media outlets, the television, movie, and music industries undoubtedly have the greatest influence on teenagers today. The goal of these corporate giants is to make a big profit. The struggle for survival in the world of entertainment has come to this: In order to stay ahead of the competition, it's imperative to deliver something new and spectacular to impress the public. And if these businesses want something to sell fast, they turn to a proven recipe for success – more violence, sex, and graphic images. They believe that they have to stimulate and raise our senses to new heights so that we will buy their products. It doesn't really matter how these things affect the audience, as long as the product is popular or "entertaining."

And what happens when the entertainment industry is criticized for its tactics? It takes the easy way out by saying, "We're just giving the public what it wants," or "We're only a mirror of society." In essence, they are saying that things are pretty rotten in our world and that we have to go to new extremes in everything we do.

It's obvious that the people who provide us with TV shows, movies, and CDs have tried to stretch our imaginations to extremes. For example, let's look at how the intensity of violence in the movies has progressed. When someone was shot in a movie in the 1950s, there was no bullet hole or blood. The guy just doubled over and slumped to the floor. Then movies began to get more realistic: a small bloodstain would appear on the victim's shirt. Then came scenes where the bullets were shown hitting the victim. Now, a shooting in a movie (and a number of TV shows) must include pools of blood, gaping wounds, gushing arteries, and so on.

Unfortunately, seeing this type of "entertainment" so often has desensitized many people to violence, both on the screen and in real life. We've become numb. Nothing shocks us anymore. Guts and gore? We've seen it before. Sex? What else can you show? Special effects? What can you do that hasn't been done before? We seem to search continually for something new.

So how far can movies, television, and music go? Is it harmful? These are interesting questions to think about. Let's take a look at some possible answers.

Who Gets Hurt?

The more people see or hear something, the more likely they are to accept it as real and let it influence their behavior. Negative messages presented in the media – images, pictures, sounds, and words – are most harmful when people become so conditioned to them that they begin to act on or act out what they see and hear. In other words, if people watch hours of TV shows or movies where someone treats others with disrespect, it's possible that those people will let that behavior become part of the relationships with others.

Let's look at areas where this could happen:

✔ **Violence.** Recent research indicates that kids who watch a lot of programs with violent material are more likely to be violent in their interactions with others than kids who aren't exposed to those kinds of programs. In one study, preschool children were more likely to hit out at their playmates, argue, disobey class rules, leave tasks unfinished, and were less willing to wait for things after watching aggressive cartoons than their counterparts who watched nonviolent programming.

Many of us have become conditioned to accept on-screen violence as entertainment. Take current music videos. Many show violence against women. The message presented here is that women are objects to be used or abused by men. Women exist to please men. Guys get the message that they should be aggressive and dominant.

✔ **Alcohol.** Another destructive message is that alcohol is the key to having fun, getting girls, and being cool. It's not. Guys who drink beer seldom get the bronzed beach babes who appear in the ads and commercials. Commercials that portray drinking as mature, sophisticated, or just good fun fail to show the harmful effects of using alcohol.

Here's some real information: Recent studies show that the more teenagers drink, the more likely they are to be victims or perpetrators of crime. Alcohol consumption is associated with 27 percent of all homicides, 31 percent of all rapes, 33 percent of all property offenses, and 37 percent of all robberies committed by young people.

Teenagers who drink are more likely to become crime victims because intoxicated people tend to provoke assailants, appear vulnerable, and fail to take normal, common sense precautions. That means if you drink, you're setting yourself up to be victimized.

✔ **Sex.** That's what life is all about, right? It's the topic of many conversations. The purpose in life is to "score," isn't it? If you like someone, it's okay to have sex, and it's probably even expected. Nobody gets hurt, and everyone has a good time, right?

That's what many movies, television shows, and songs would have you think. The truth is that the number of teenagers who get pregnant or contract sexually transmitted diseases is skyrocketing. The truth is that reported cases of date violence and date rape are on the rise. In one survey of high school students, one of five girls and two of five boys said they thought it was okay to force sex on a girl if she is drunk. It is not okay. It is rape. It is a terrible physical and emotional crime.

Then there's the issue of sex being portrayed as nothing more than a physical act for temporary pleasure, when it should be part of a loving relationship between a man and woman who are married.

What does this have to do with teenage relationships? Teenagers can lose track of what's right with their lives if they can't or don't separate the good messages from the bad. Possibly the biggest mistake the media make is showing that people can commit harmful, violent, illegal, or immoral acts without suffering any consequences. There are few consequences for the movie hero who blows someone away with a machine gun or breaks a neck with a karate chop. After all, the star has to appear in a sequel. No one gets hurt from sexual relations. People don't suffer when they use alcohol and drugs. These are the messages some people receive. The opposite is true. There are consequences, and they are severe.

For people who don't have a conscience – leading a life that doesn't value or respect what's right and moral, or not caring when they do something wrong – the media can have a profound effect. They will act out the messages they see and hear, regardless of whether they hurt themselves or others in the process.

Not everyone is like that, of course. But you have to be aware of the impact these messages can have on others. For example, you may be strong enough and aware enough to resist the images, but what about someone several years younger than you? What about a little sister or brother who hears and sees these messages? It won't be long until you are an adult and have the responsibility of teaching and taking care of the next generation. What will you tell them to believe?

What's Real and What's Not?

Much of what the media tries to sell is their vision of the "perfect" lifestyle. Television, movies, and music present messages that tell people how they should think or act if they really want to enjoy life to its fullest. And even though most of us think we're simply being entertained, these messages are always being peddled to us. Sometimes they are direct; sometimes they are hidden.

For example, messages aimed at teenagers frequently tell them that being cool means doing whatever feels good. Men are usually portrayed as tough, macho, aggressive, and able to get any woman they want. Women are portrayed as sexy, passive and weak—love goddesses or sex slaves.

Lifestyles – usually wild ones – are popular topics for television talk shows and magazine articles. The messages: Go where the action is. Bizarre is beautiful. Walk on the wild side. The more outrageous the behaviors, the better the chances of drawing an audience.

Athletes, musicians, and movie stars also tell of their sexual escapades or drug habits. Living life "on the edge" is viewed as exciting and exotic. Here they are, idolized by many people, talking and laughing about the "crazy" things they did. And even though their lives may have been torn apart by their lack of self-control, society clamors to hear more. There is something fascinating about celebrity "bad boys" and "bad girls." People pay attention.

And what about TV sitcoms? Many feature families in which wisecracking, super-hip kids have a line for everything. They act in illegal or immoral ways but still get out of any predicament. They become trend-setters for clothing and hairstyles. More important, the way they treat people on their shows becomes a model for the way real kids treat others. Catch phrases or mannerisms used by the show's youthful star quickly become part of young people's language. And isn't it interesting that no matter how monumental the problems presented in these shows, they can always be solved in thirty minutes.

Lifestyles created by the media also involve sexual images. One study estimates that in a single year, TV alone airs 20,000 sexual messages. There's not much that could be more harmful to young people's moral development than believing that having sex requires no more emotional involvement than brushing their teeth.

▼
● *If God had believed in permissiveness, He would have given us the Ten Suggestions.*

The Language of Disrespect

Everyone wants to be treated with respect. Look at the messages you get from some TV shows, movies, and music. Many show disrespect. The messages say that it's okay to "get in someone's face" if he or she disagrees with you, or that you have a right to be cruel to other people if they are different.

A Media Message Exercise

Watch your regular TV shows, listen to your favorite radio station, or go to a popular movie. Then answer the following questions about the messages you received:

✔ How many messages told you to worry only about yourself rather than care about others? How many told you to "do your own thing" without worrying about others?

✔ How many people were put down, made fun of, or hurt by insensitive words or actions? How many times did this happen?

✔ How did men and women or boys and girls treat each other? As equals? As friends? As

116

enemies or stereotypes? Did they treat each other with respect or sarcasm?

✔ How many messages stressed responsibility and doing the right thing?

✔ How many times did you see anger or violence?

✔ How many times were drugs mentioned or used?

✔ How many references were there to sex?

If you are able to sift through all you see and hear and make some sense of it, more power to you. Many people just absorb the messages without thinking.

Most people, teens included, believe in traditional values – a loving family, a good job, a nice home. But values such as moderation, love, commitment, faith, respect, and sensitivity are boring to the people who create the entertainment we watch. There aren't many TV shows or movies about solid marriages or healthy relationships. They won't draw big audiences and big profits. And it doesn't appear that the media are going to change to accommodate the part of society that would like to see these values presented more often and more honestly.

Stand by Your Values

What can you and other teenagers do to protect yourselves and develop positive values? Here are some suggestions:

1 **Set and keep safe standards for yourself.** Know who you are, and know what is really important to you. Know what you like, what you will tolerate from others, and what makes you feel good about yourself. If it's different from what the media says is cool, so what? Don't let TV shows, movies, and advertisements convince you that it's okay to do something you know isn't right just to be accepted. If a TV show or commercial is funny or exciting, that's fine. Laugh at it, and enjoy it, but don't live it.

2 **Don't buy the media's message that sex is the same thing as love.** The simplest animal is capable of having sex, but it's not capable of knowing what love is. If a date tries to talk you into having sex because he or she believes the image that "everybody's doing it," that's wrong. Two people can love each other without having sex, despite what you might see or hear in the media and from other teens. Girls especially need to be strong in the face of what the media portray as ideal female images and the casual attitude toward sex.

3 **Don't buy the media's message that the way to get what you want is through violence and aggression.** People don't have to hurt one another to get what is good in life.

4 **Observe positive role models.** There are many athletes, actors, and musicians who are giving you good messages. Listen to them, and make your own choices. Think for yourself. And stand up for the choices you make. Enjoy all of the wonderful things that the media can give you, but turn a deaf ear to messages that promote unhealthy thinking.

5 **Enjoy entertainment for what it is worth.** A break from reality is healthy sometimes. But stick to what you know is right. And make the best of your life. For real.

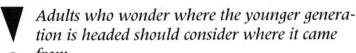 *Adults who wonder where the younger generation is headed should consider where it came from.*

Being in Love

Most people will experience the tremendously powerful and complex emotion called "love."

We have a love affair with love. What topic comes up more in our society? The word itself flows through our language. Listen to the many ways love affects our lives. It can make us any or all of the following:

✔ athletic – "head over heels in love"

✔ visually impaired – "blinded by love"

✔ visually gifted – "love at first sight"

✔ buy houses – "our little love-nest"

✔ target of insects – "bitten by the love-bug"

✔ unhealthy – "she's lovesick"

✔ care for animals – "puppy love"

✔ believe it will last forever – "endless love, undying love, eternal love"

Wow! What other word has been used in so many different ways? "Love" is used in so many ways that we casually throw it around: He loves his car. She loves her hair. He loves football. She loves pizza and ice cream. There's a mother's love and brotherly love. We're supposed to love our neighbor. When the word is used in these ways, it only means that a person cares a great deal about something or someone. It has nothing to do with mature, romantic love.

▎▶ Kevin's Story

Kevin and Lisa, who are now juniors in high school, have been going together to school functions and other activities since they were in eighth grade. To the other kids, they seem inseparable; they spend all their time together. Kevin is crazy about Lisa. He gave her a ring for her birthday and thinks she is the most beautiful girl in the world. Lisa, on the other hand, feels safe and comfortable and considers Kevin her closest friend.

This year, everything changed. A new guy, Rob, moved to the area and began attending their school. Lisa was attracted to him immediately. She told Kevin about it and said that she wanted to be Kevin's friend, but only his friend. She's now going out with Rob. Kevin was crushed; he thought his relationship with Lisa was forever. He doesn't know if he should turn his back on Lisa or try to get even. Maybe, he thinks, he should wait it out or try to get her back. He's hurt and angry and doesn't know how to respond. He is sure he'll never get over this pain.

Real Love or Infatuation?

When you are infatuated with someone, it means you are intensely attracted to that individual. Many people refer to this as having a "crush" on someone. The infatuated person usually puts the other person on a pedestal and overlooks his or her faults because of the overwhelming attraction.

Infatuation usually begins with an attraction to some characteristic that you see and like right away – a good body, pretty eyes, neat hair, a sexy walk, or a friendly smile. You may experience a funny feeling in the pit of your stomach. You may think you can't be around this person enough, or you may be "swept off your feet" by the other person's charm. In fact, you can be so taken by this attraction that you don't pay much attention to the whole person. And you'll probably think you're in love.

This doesn't mean that you don't have affection for that person. But infatuation usually disappears as quickly as it appears. It's like a flaming meteor that burns red-hot, and then quickly dies. This type of "love":

✔ is emotionally exhausting.

✔ makes you daydream a lot.

✔ distracts you at work or in school.

✔ makes you act irresponsibly.

✔ makes you jealous or possessive.

✔ takes your energy away.

So if you think you're in love but act irresponsibly or even destructively, it's much more likely that you're infatuated.

What Is Real Love?

Love is difficult to define and too complex to explain clearly. Poets, authors, and songwriters have tried for years to pin down what love is, and no one has succeeded. Of course, if you use TV soap operas and movies as your "guide to love," you're bound to be confused. They usually follow a basic formula: As soon as two people see one another, they "know." Sparks fly when they first touch. They fall madly and passionately into the greatest and deepest love a man and a woman have ever known. Nothing will stand between them – not land mines, nuclear war, terminal illness, bloodthirsty aliens, killer tomatoes, or earthquakes. No obstacle is too great to keep them apart: neither land nor sea nor rival governments.

Unlike the scripts in romantic movies or soap operas, real love doesn't have quite the same pizzazz. The feelings of love can be deep and intense; in fact, they can be very similar to the feelings of infatuation. But infatuation makes it seem like you're walking around in a blurry dream; love lets you see clearly. And the biggest difference between the two is that love stands the test of time while infatuation fades quickly.

▼ *Respect is love in plain clothes.*

Real love is based on friendship, trust, and concern for the other person. Love focuses on the whole person and all of his or her qualities, not simply the physical equipment. It's liking the "outside" of a person, but liking what's "inside" even more. Physical appearances and attractiveness are like the pretty wrapping on Christmas presents; they merely hold the real gift.

Teenagers shouldn't spend their time looking for their "one and only." They would be on a wild goose chase. You can't force love; you have to let it develop over time.

You probably will be attracted to at least one person during your teenage years. Even though this person may not be the one you will eventually marry, you can enjoy an appropriate love that is good for you at this stage of your life. This kind of love energizes you and keeps your life headed in the right direction. This type of love means that you accept the other person, faults and all. It is constructive and non-possessive. It helps each partner become a better person. This type of love prepares you for mature love, a love you will feel later in your life, a love that makes you ready for marriage.

Appropriate love is healthy for you. The girl doesn't have to "give" herself to the boy. The boy isn't after the girl only to satisfy a physical desire. Both people respect and like each other and enjoy being around one another in a sharing, caring relationship. They bring out the best in one another.

Appropriate love . . .

✔ gives you confidence and makes you feel good.

✔ allows two people to build a friendship based on caring for one another.

✔ focuses you.

✔ energizes you.

✔ helps you to be more responsible.

✔ helps you do better at your job and at school.

✔ lets two people enjoy being together.

✔ doesn't upset you, even when your loved one isn't around.

Stop in the Name of Love

If your love relationship doesn't energize you in the right direction, it's not appropriate love. Being energized in the right direction means doing your best in your studies, activities, and relationships with your parents and friends. If you're so focused on one person that you've started forgetting or putting off responsibilities, it might be a good idea to put the relationship on hold or drop it altogether.

When you fall in love this way, it doesn't mean anything more than you fell in love. This may seem rather cold, but it's not meant to be. Most people fall in love during their lives, some many times. That doesn't mean that what they're experiencing is real love; they are just "in love." There is a big difference between the two.

People tend to get impatient when they are in love. You know what that's like, don't you? You can't wait to be with the other person. Your heart starts to pound, and you're tingling with excitement. Those are neat feelings to have.

However, when a person starts agonizing over what the other person is doing, or wonders constantly when he or she is going to call or write, and thinks about the person continually, it can be unhealthy. The person might begin to shirk his or her responsibilities, or become jealous or demanding.

You shouldn't drop all of your other relationships and interests to pursue someone you think you love. You shouldn't change your whole life to please another person. That's the stuff you'll find in those shows and books. And while it makes good viewing and reading, in reality it can really mess up your life. When the relationship breaks up, the person who did all the worrying and changing is left alone.

This is not to make you feel like a special relationship you might have now is silly or meaningless; on the contrary, it is important and meaningful. If it is healthy and makes you happy, that's wonderful. Just make sure that the things you do for a relationship don't keep you from taking care of your responsibilities and becoming a better person. Don't worry about whether this relationship will turn into something special. If it's real love, it will flourish. For the time being, enjoy yourself and your special someone. Have fun with your friends, and let everything fall into place.

Breaking Up Is Hard to Do

Many teen dating relationships break up. When they do, it's a big hurt for someone. It's not unusual for one or both people to lose the passion and excitement they once felt. It means they probably just had a crush on each other. When the newness wears off, behavior that used to be cute or attractive starts to get a little annoying. People begin to see qualities that they don't like, and whatever attracted them in the first place loses its power. Dates become boring. These are good indicators that a relationship wasn't supposed to become a long-term commitment.

When a relationship breaks up, you or the person you were dating may be depressed and sad because something special has ended. There may even be a period of mourning because the relationship that you thought was special is now over. Breaking up really is hard to do. And it's not as if you immediately stop caring for each other; deep feelings don't dissolve into thin air. You still care in some ways. You just don't care as much or as passionately as before.

If something like this happens to you, you're better off agreeing to be good friends and dating other people. As you grow and mature, you will sometimes change your opinions of what and whom you think are important.

It's important to remember that falling in love and ending a romantic relationship are parts of the growing-up process. All your relationships and "loves" will help you find the person you really love. It's almost like taking a series of pop quizzes so you can pass the final test. You learn a little more each time you fall in love.

Healthy relationships rely on talking and sharing and caring. If you're not actively doing something to make a relationship better or you feel you just don't care anymore, there is little hope that it will survive. It is better to end it as positively as you can and move on.

People frequently try to hold on a little longer; they avoid the truth by hoping that everything will work out. They don't want to hurt the other person, but they know their feelings aren't as deep as they used to be. It's unlikely that things will work out on their own. Some people think that having sex will make everything better. It doesn't; it only complicates matters. Relationships built solely on sex or a sexual attraction don't last. And losing a relationship isn't as serious as losing your self-respect and happiness. It's important to remember that you can break up with someone and survive. In fact, what you learn may make you stronger and improve your future relationships. This may be far from your mind at the time of a break-up, but you will decide to take the risk again.

When your friends or parents say that you'll get over it, they're not being sarcastic, uncaring, or unsympathetic. In all likelihood, they're right. You will get over it. If you have ever been hurt because a relationship broke up, you know that all the encouraging words and logical thinking in the world couldn't make you feel better. It didn't make any difference what people said; you still felt bad. Healing any hurt takes time; it's not different with romantic hurt. But dwelling on the pain you feel doesn't help, either. You have to get on with your life.

▼ *We may give without loving, but we cannot love*
● *without giving.*

Real love involves giving as much as getting. There are rough times that you must face together. Love is realizing that no one is perfect and being able to live with another person's imperfections. True love is based on a commitment to one another – working together toward common goals and interests. There are great times. You will cherish the love you have together. But getting through the tough times together is the glue that holds strong relationships together.

▼ *Marriage is not a destination; it is a journey.*
●

Marriage

Most teens don't think much about marriage. It's light-years away from where they are today, and it's not something they should be overly concerned with at this point in their lives.

But someday you will fall in love – real love. Being with just that one person will sound perfect. You will start talking about marriage. There are many things to think about before you make what could be the biggest decision of your life.

Marriage is lifelong partnership. A man and woman have to work at making a marriage successful; it doesn't just happen. And while there are no guarantees for success, knowing what to look for in a partner can help you find someone who is right for you.

Here are several things to consider:

1 Communication. When two people get married, they have to learn how to live together. If they can talk openly – not just when things are going well, but in all situations – they have a better chance of surviving the hard times. One person may not always say things the other person wants to hear, but openness in a relationship is extremely important. In fact, resentment grows when marriage partners keep their feelings to themselves. The frustration can eventually build to a point where both people are unhappy.

132

2 Certainty. Don't rush into a relationship. Learn as much as you can about the other person. See how he or she acts in a variety of places and situations. Many marriages fail because one partner sees a side of his or her spouse that wasn't revealed before they were married. Know how a person acts when he or she is mad, frustrated, bored, happy, or sad. Look at the many sides of the person's personality. Look at the way he or she treats others.

One of the reasons marriages fail is that both the people rely entirely on the feelings they had for each other during their dating relationship. When people date, they try to make everything perfect. They are on their best behavior – charming, warm, loving – and the focus of dating is to have a good time. When two people marry, there are all kinds of situations they have to handle together, and they are not always enjoyable. A person finds that his or her spouse has annoying habits. That's why it is so important for two people to get to know each other very well. Choosing a mate for life is serious business; it's not something to take lightly.

So the next time you feel that you've found "the real thing," stop and think a minute. It may be hard to stop your feelings, but you can stop your actions. True love is permanent and gets stronger, not weaker. Just because you may feel turned on when the other person is around, don't mistake that feeling for true love. The basis for true love is friendship. So take it slowly. Don't go too far, too fast. If it's love, it will stand the test of time.

 The goal of marriage is not to think alike, but to think together.

★
Choice and Change

Throughout this book, you have been encouraged to meet new people, to develop positive relationships, and to make the most of your abilities. This involves taking some risks along the way and always putting forth your best effort. If you learn to treat mistakes and failures simply as invitations to try again, you are more likely to accomplish your goals. You see, there isn't any map for the road to success; you have to find your own way.

> ▼ *A few may strike it rich, but we'd*
> *Accept it on authority*
> *That if at first you don't succeed*
> ● *You're with the vast majority.*

Although this book has concentrated mostly on helping you learn appropriate skills for getting along with others, there also were some warnings about the harmful aspects of relationships. There are some risks you shouldn't take. Some people are like the moon; there's a dark side that they keep hidden from sight. There are people you shouldn't trust and some you should avoid altogether. And you can't fight the enemy unless you can identify the enemy.

▼ *The dictionary is the only place where success*
● *comes before work.*

For the most part, however, this book is aimed at helping you to be successful in friendships. When you take time to look back and sum up the experiences you've had as a teenager, you are likely to find that positive relationships and good friends gave you the most satisfying moments of your life. If you can be successful with relationships, you can be successful with living. It's that simple. Learning how to get along with others puts you a step ahead of those people who don't even try. You will not only accomplish many of your goals, you'll also enjoy your life much more.

Although some of the choices you make will be difficult, it is important to continue to believe in yourself and your abilities. There's no answer sheet to the test of life. You have to figure out each problem as you live each day of your life. Learning from successes as well as failures makes you a more complete person. It's when you don't learn that you truly fail. So don't be afraid of making decisions and taking some chances; just take some time to think and plan before you act.

Most of the choices you make in your life should be based on the concern you have for others and yourself. Having a deep respect for doing what is good for you and others should be a guiding force in your life. Within each of us is something worth sharing with others. Keep an open mind. Learn all you can. As you learn, you will find new talents and interests just waiting to blossom. Good luck and have a happy life.

Live Each Day to Its Fullest

Live each day to its fullest. Get the most from each hour, each day, and each age of your life. Then you can look forward with confidence, and back without regrets.

Be yourself – but be your best self. Dare to be different and follow your own star.

Don't be afraid to be happy. Enjoy what is beautiful.

Love with all your heart and soul. And believe that those you love, love you.

Forget what you have done for your friends, and remember what they have done for you.

Disregard what the world owes you and concentrate instead on what you owe the world.

When you are faced with a decision, make that decision as wisely as possible – then forget it. The moment of absolute truth never arrives.

Remember above all that God helps those who help themselves. Act as if everything depended on you, and pray as if everything depended on God.